THE SECRET IS OUT

William Stanek is the artist behind the scenes at World Galleries, and the fiction author Robert Stanek.

BW Fall Arrives at Multnomah Falls in Canvas Print with Floating Frame

Find his art at 360 Studios

360studios.pictorem.com

williamrstanek.com

Note About the Front Matter

The front matter serves as an essential foundation for the series, ensuring that all readers—whether new to the books or returning after some time—can fully grasp the material. It introduces key concepts like the 8 Pillars of Intelligence and the Holistic Intelligence Model, both developed by William Stanek, providing critical context and continuity across the series. This consistent framework enables readers to engage deeply with the content, regardless of where they begin in the series.

For readers already familiar with these concepts, the option to skip directly to the main content is always available, allowing them to dive right into the heart of the book. This structure ensures accessibility for all, while respecting the time of experienced readers.

The Holistic Intelligence Model: The 8 Pillars of Personal and Professional Excellence

The 8 Pillars of Intelligence form the foundation of the Holistic Intelligence Model developed by William Stanek, a transformative framework designed to empower individuals in every dimension of life. This model transcends traditional notions of intelligence by encompassing eight distinct yet interconnected pillars: Emotional Resilience, Creativity Intelligence, Practical Intelligence, Cultural Intelligence, Intrapersonal Intelligence, Interpersonal Intelligence, Ethical Intelligence, and Analytical Intelligence. Each pillar represents a crucial dimension of human capability, addressing intellectual, emotional, ethical, and social competencies essential for thriving in today's dynamic and interconnected world.

At its core, the Holistic Intelligence Model emphasizes the synergy between these eight pillars, recognizing that true excellence arises from the harmonious development of diverse intelligences. By fostering resilience, creativity, practical problem-solving, cultural adaptability, self-awareness, interpersonal skills, ethical grounding, and analytical prowess, individuals are empowered to navigate complex challenges, build meaningful relationships, and achieve sustained success. This comprehensive approach ensures that personal growth is balanced across multiple facets of intelligence, promoting not only professional achievements but also overall well-being and fulfillment.

The model serves as a foundational guide for individuals seeking to enhance their capabilities in a structured and systematic manner. It provides actionable strategies and development pathways for each pillar, enabling continuous improvement and integration of these intelligences into daily life. Whether in leadership roles, creative endeavors, or personal relationships, the Holistic Intelligence Model equips individuals with the tools necessary to excel holistically, fostering a resilient, innovative, and ethically grounded mindset that drives meaningful impact and lasting success.

Pillar 1: Emotional Resilience (ER)

Emotional Resilience (ER) is the foundational pillar of the Holistic Intelligence Model, embodying the capacity to withstand and recover from emotional challenges and setbacks. It equips individuals with the strength to navigate adversity, maintain composure under pressure, and sustain a positive outlook despite difficulties. ER is not merely about bouncing back; it is about growing stronger and more adaptable through life's inevitable trials, thereby fostering long-term psychological well-being and stability.

The significance of Emotional Resilience extends across personal and professional domains. In the workplace, ER enhances performance by enabling individuals to manage stress effectively, stay focused on long-term goals, and lead teams with confidence during crises. Personally, it strengthens relationships by promoting empathy, effective communication, and the ability to support oneself and others through tough times. By cultivating ER, individuals build a robust emotional foundation that supports perseverance, adaptability, and proactive problem-solving, essential traits for sustained success and fulfillment.

Developing Emotional Resilience involves intentional practices such as mindfulness, self-compassion, and building strong social support networks. Strategies include embracing a growth mindset, enhancing coping skills through physical activity and stress management techniques, and fostering self-awareness through reflective practices. Practical applications of ER range from handling workplace stress and leading teams with composure to managing personal challenges and maintaining healthy relationships. By integrating ER with other intelligences, individuals can achieve a balanced and resilient approach to both personal growth and professional excellence.

Pillar 2: Creativity Intelligence (CrQ)

Creativity Intelligence (CrQ) is the pillar that fuels innovation, enabling individuals to generate unique ideas, solve problems innovatively, and adapt to changing environments with a creative mindset. CrQ encompasses a range of cognitive and emotional skills that facilitate the creation and implementation of novel concepts, processes, and products. It is essential for personal fulfillment and organizational success, fostering a culture of continuous improvement and adaptability.

The significance of Creativity Intelligence lies in its ability to drive progress and competitive advantage. In professional settings, CrQ leads to the development of new products, services, and processes that can differentiate an organization in the market. It enhances problem-solving by allowing individuals to approach challenges from unconventional angles, leading to more effective and sustainable solutions. Personally, CrQ contributes to a sense of achievement and satisfaction by enabling individuals to express their creativity and pursue innovative interests.

Enhancing Creativity Intelligence involves cultivating an explorative mindset, fostering adaptive thinking, and strengthening problem-solving proficiency. Strategies include engaging in creative activities, embracing playfulness, practicing divergent thinking, and seeking inspiration from diverse sources. Practical applications of CrQ range from leading innovation projects and strategic planning in the workplace to pursuing creative hobbies and personal goals in everyday life. By integrating CrQ with other intelligences, individuals can harness their creative potential to achieve both personal growth and professional excellence.

Pillar 3: Practical Intelligence (PQ)

Practical Intelligence (PQ), often referred to as "street smarts," is the ability to apply knowledge effectively in real-world situations. It bridges the gap between theoretical understanding and practical application, enabling individuals to navigate everyday complexities with confidence and efficiency. PQ encompasses skills such as effective decision-making, resource management, and adaptability, which are crucial for achieving tangible outcomes in both personal and professional contexts.

The significance of Practical Intelligence is evident in its impact on efficiency and effectiveness. In the workplace, PQ enhances project management, streamlines business processes, and supports strategic planning by ensuring that ideas are implemented successfully. It empowers individuals to solve problems pragmatically, optimize resources, and adapt to changing circumstances, thereby increasing productivity and reducing operational costs. Personally, PQ facilitates effective time management, financial planning, and home organization, contributing to a balanced and organized lifestyle.

Developing Practical Intelligence involves enhancing adaptability and flexibility, strengthening problem-solving and decision-making skills, and improving resource management and optimization. Strategies include engaging in scenario planning, utilizing decision-making frameworks, and practicing continuous improvement techniques. Practical applications of PQ range from managing business operations and executing strategic plans in the workplace to organizing daily tasks and achieving personal financial goals. By integrating PQ with other intelligences, individuals can ensure that their practical skills support their overall growth and success.

Pillar 4: Cultural Intelligence (CQ)

Cultural Intelligence (CQ) is the capability to relate and work effectively across diverse cultural settings. In an increasingly globalized world, CQ is essential for navigating multicultural environments, fostering inclusive workplaces, and building strong, respectful relationships with individuals from different cultural backgrounds. It involves understanding cultural norms, values, and communication styles, and adapting one's behavior to fit various cultural contexts.

The significance of Cultural Intelligence extends to both personal enrichment and professional success. In the workplace, CQ facilitates effective teamwork and collaboration in multicultural teams, enhances cross-cultural communication, and supports market expansion into new regions by understanding local consumer behaviors and business practices. Personally, CQ enriches interactions by promoting mutual respect, reducing misunderstandings, and fostering meaningful relationships with people from diverse backgrounds. It also contributes to personal growth by broadening perspectives and enhancing global awareness.

Enhancing Cultural Intelligence involves increasing cultural awareness, improving adaptability and flexibility, and developing empathy and social competence. Strategies include cultural education, immersion experiences, active listening, and empathy exercises. Practical applications of CQ range from leading multicultural teams and expanding businesses into international markets to building intercultural friendships and participating in diverse community activities. By integrating CQ with other intelligences, individuals can navigate cultural complexities with ease, fostering a harmonious and inclusive environment in all areas of life.

Pillar 5: Intrapersonal Intelligence (IntraQ)

Intrapersonal Intelligence (IntraQ), also known as Reflective Intelligence, is the capacity to understand oneself deeply. It encompasses self-awareness, self-regulation, and the ability to reflect on one's thoughts, emotions, and motivations. IntraQ is fundamental for personal growth, effective decision-making, and aligning actions with personal values and goals, providing a strong foundation for overall well-being and fulfillment.

The significance of Intrapersonal Intelligence lies in its role in fostering self-understanding and personal development. In the workplace, IntraQ enhances leadership by enabling leaders to understand their strengths and weaknesses, manage their emotions, and make decisions that are aligned with their values. It supports career development by helping individuals set clear goals and pursue them with intentionality and self-discipline. Personally, IntraQ contributes to emotional well-being by promoting self-compassion, resilience, and the ability to navigate personal challenges with clarity and purpose.

Developing Intrapersonal Intelligence involves cultivating self-awareness, enhancing emotional regulation, and fostering personal growth and self-reflection. Strategies include journaling, mindfulness meditation, and engaging in reflective practices that promote introspection and self-assessment. Practical applications of IntraQ range from setting and achieving personal goals and managing stress effectively to maintaining authentic relationships and pursuing continuous self-improvement. By integrating IntraQ with other intelligences, individuals can achieve a balanced and insightful approach to personal and professional excellence, ensuring that their actions are purposeful and aligned with their core values.

Pillar 6: Interpersonal Intelligence (InterQ)

Interpersonal Intelligence (InterQ), also known as Social Intelligence, is the ability to understand, communicate, and interact effectively with others. It involves recognizing and interpreting the emotions, motivations, and intentions of others, facilitating meaningful relationships and effective collaboration. InterQ is essential for leadership, teamwork, conflict resolution, and building a supportive social network, making it a critical component of the Holistic Intelligence Model.

The significance of Interpersonal Intelligence is evident in its impact on both personal relationships and professional environments. In the workplace, InterQ enhances team dynamics, fosters collaboration, and supports effective leadership by enabling individuals to inspire and motivate others. It facilitates client relations, conflict management, and networking, contributing to a positive and productive work culture. Personally, InterQ strengthens friendships, family bonds, and community connections by promoting empathy, effective communication, and mutual understanding, leading to more fulfilling and harmonious relationships.

Enhancing Interpersonal Intelligence involves developing empathy and social awareness, improving communication skills, and strengthening conflict management and negotiation abilities. Strategies include active listening, empathy exercises, and engaging in collaborative and team-building activities. Practical applications of InterQ range from leading diverse teams and building strong client relationships in the workplace to maintaining healthy friendships and family relationships in personal life. By integrating InterQ with other intelligences, individuals can foster a supportive and engaging social environment, enhancing both their personal well-being and professional success.

Pillar 7: Ethical Intelligence (EthQ)

Ethical Intelligence (EthQ) serves as the moral compass within the Holistic Intelligence Model, guiding individuals in making principled choices and maintaining integrity in all aspects of life. It involves understanding and adhering to ethical standards, promoting fairness, and demonstrating accountability and responsibility. EthQ is essential for building trust, fostering a positive reputation, and leading with integrity, ensuring that actions are aligned with moral values and societal expectations.

The significance of Ethical Intelligence is profound in both personal and professional contexts. In the workplace, EthQ enhances leadership by promoting ethical decision-making, integrity, and accountability, which are crucial for building trust and credibility within teams and organizations. It supports the development and enforcement of ethical policies, contributing to a culture of responsibility and fairness. Personally, EthQ ensures that individuals uphold their values in their interactions and decisions, fostering honest and trustworthy relationships and contributing positively to their communities.

Developing Ethical Intelligence involves clarifying personal values, enhancing ethical decision-making skills, and fostering integrity and accountability. Strategies include values clarification exercises, utilizing ethical decision-making frameworks, and engaging in continuous ethical education and reflection. Practical applications of EthQ range from leading with integrity and developing ethical policies in the workplace to maintaining honesty and fairness in personal relationships and community engagements. By integrating EthQ with other intelligences, individuals can ensure that their actions are not only effective and innovative but also morally sound and socially responsible, leading to sustained trust and respect.

Pillar 8: Analytical Intelligence (AQ)

Analytical Intelligence (AQ) is the ability to analyze complex problems, think critically, and make informed decisions based on evidence and logical reasoning. It involves breaking down information into manageable parts, identifying patterns, and synthesizing data to derive meaningful conclusions. AQ is essential for effective problem-solving, strategic planning, and informed decision-making in both personal and professional contexts, providing the cognitive tools necessary to navigate and excel in a data-driven world.

The significance of Analytical Intelligence lies in its role in enhancing decision-making and strategic thinking. In the workplace, AQ supports strategic planning by enabling individuals to analyze market trends, assess risks, and develop data-driven strategies that align with organizational goals. It enhances problem-solving capabilities by facilitating the identification of root causes and the development of effective solutions. Personally, AQ contributes to financial management, health tracking, and educational pursuits by enabling individuals to interpret data accurately and make informed decisions that promote well-being and success.

Developing Analytical Intelligence involves enhancing critical thinking, improving problem-solving skills, and strengthening data analysis and interpretation abilities. Strategies include engaging in critical thinking exercises, utilizing data analysis tools and software, and practicing reflective journaling on problem-solving experiences. Practical applications of AQ range from strategic business expansion and process optimization in the workplace to personal financial planning and health management in everyday life. By integrating AQ with other intelligences, individuals can ensure that their analytical capabilities support comprehensive and balanced growth, enabling them to make informed, ethical, and effective decisions across all areas of life.

Conclusion

The Holistic Intelligence Model offers a comprehensive and integrated approach to personal and professional development by encompassing eight pivotal pillars: Emotional Resilience, Creativity Intelligence, Practical Intelligence, Cultural Intelligence, Intrapersonal Intelligence, Interpersonal

Intelligence, Ethical Intelligence, and Analytical Intelligence. Each pillar addresses distinct aspects of human capability, ensuring that individuals develop a balanced and multifaceted intelligence that supports resilience, innovation, ethical integrity, and effective communication. This holistic framework recognizes the interconnectedness of diverse intelligences, emphasizing that true excellence is achieved through the harmonious growth of all these dimensions.

By cultivating each of these eight pillars, individuals are empowered to navigate complex challenges, build meaningful relationships, and achieve sustained success and fulfillment. The model provides actionable strategies and development pathways, enabling continuous improvement and the integration of these intelligences into daily life. Whether in leadership roles, creative endeavors, or personal relationships, the Holistic Intelligence Model equips individuals with the tools necessary to excel holistically, fostering a resilient, innovative, and ethically grounded mindset.

Ultimately, the Holistic Intelligence Model serves as a guiding framework for individuals seeking to enhance their capabilities in a structured and systematic manner. By embracing and developing each pillar, individuals can achieve comprehensive intelligence and excellence, leading to meaningful impact and lasting success in all areas of life. Embrace this model as a transformative journey towards balanced growth, personal fulfillment, and professional achievement.

Letter from the Author

In the realm of leadership and intelligence, there exists a tapestry woven from the threads of experience, wisdom, and an unyielding commitment to excellence. This tapestry has been crafted over the course of three decades, each thread representing a moment of triumph, a lesson learned, or a challenge met head-on. It is a privilege to share these threads with you, dear reader, as we embark on a journey through the corridors of leadership, guided by the principles of the Holistic Intelligence Model.

In these pages, you will discover not only a roadmap to effective leadership but also a comprehensive framework that integrates Emotional Resilience, Creativity Intelligence,

Practical Intelligence, Cultural Intelligence, Intrapersonal Intelligence, Interpersonal Intelligence, Ethical Intelligence, and Analytical Intelligence. These eight pillars form the foundation of a multifaceted intelligence that transcends traditional measures, enabling leaders to navigate complex landscapes with adaptability, innovation, and integrity.

As we delve into the nuances of each pillar, you will gain insights into how these interconnected intelligences work in synergy to foster resilient and dynamic leadership. Whether it's harnessing Emotional Resilience to maintain composure under pressure, leveraging Creativity Intelligence to drive innovation, or applying Ethical Intelligence to uphold integrity, each pillar offers practical strategies and profound wisdom. Together, they unlock doors to innovation, adaptability, and enduring success, providing a holistic approach to leadership that is both practical and inspiring.

This book is not merely a collection of ideas but a distillation of a lifetime's worth of experiences, framed within the Holistic Intelligence Model. It is an offering to leaders, both seasoned and aspiring, who seek to cultivate a balanced and integrated intelligence that supports sustained excellence and fulfillment. It is my sincerest hope that you will find within these pages not only practical guidance but also inspiration to lead with purpose, passion, and resilience, embodying the essence of holistic intelligence in every endeavor.

In the crucible of leadership, one discovers not only the power to guide and influence but also the profound responsibility that comes with it. Over three decades at the intersection of technology, business, and leadership, I have gleaned insights that have shaped my approach to leadership intelligence. From navigating pivotal historical moments to addressing complex technological challenges, these experiences have reinforced the importance of a balanced and integrated intelligence framework.

Throughout my career as a technology consultant and leader, I have learned that the heart of many seemingly insurmountable problems lies not in technological failings but in the nuanced dynamics of leadership and intelligence. This revelation became the cornerstone of my approach, emphasizing that effective leadership is a multifaceted endeavor encompassing Emotional Resilience, Practical Intelligence, Ethical Intelligence, and the other pillars of holistic intelligence. By embracing this integrated framework, leaders can inspire, influence, and adeptly guide teams through even the most formidable challenges.

In this book, and indeed throughout this series, I invite you to embark on a journey of discovery, exploring the intricacies of leading with purpose, adaptability, and a commitment to growth. Together, we will harness the power of holistic intelligence to achieve greater effectiveness, impact, and resilience. May these pages serve as a compass on your own leadership journey, guiding you towards balanced growth and meaningful success.

With warm regards,

William R. Stanek.

Our Foundational Proposition: Navigating the Complex Tapestry of Success

In a world saturated with discussions on various intelligences, our perspective transcends the oversimplified dichotomy of emotional intelligence (EQ) versus intellectual intelligence (IQ). While acknowledging the undeniable importance of emotional intelligence, our exploration delves deeper, recognizing the intricate interplay of the eight pillars of the Holistic Intelligence Model—Emotional Resilience, Creativity Intelligence, Practical Intelligence, Cultural Intelligence, Intrapersonal Intelligence, Interpersonal Intelligence, Ethical Intelligence, and Analytical Intelligence—within the tapestry of effective living and success.

Consider the story of Temple Grandin, a renowned scientist and advocate for individuals with autism. Her unique perspective and creative problem-solving have revolutionized the livestock industry. Grandin's journey reflects the intersection of Practical Intelligence, Emotional Resilience, and Creativity Intelligence, showcasing the versatile dimensions crucial for life, success, and leadership. Similarly, visionaries like Elon Musk demonstrate the indispensable role of Practical Intelligence and Analytical Intelligence in achieving monumental feats. Musk's relentless commitment to innovation highlights how these intelligences synergize to propel progress, rather than overshadow one another.

Meet Frances Arnold, a groundbreaking chemist and engineer awarded the Nobel Prize in Chemistry. Her journey of innovation showcases not only Analytical Intelligence but also Emotional Resilience in a field where women were historically underrepresented. Arnold's creative problem-solving and tenacity redefine the boundaries of intelligence in life, success, and leadership, embodying the harmonious blend of multiple intelligences that drive profound achievements. Steve Jobs, with his unparalleled Analytical Acumen and Creativity Intelligence, demonstrated that visionary success goes beyond emotional intelligence. His ability to distill complex ideas into user-friendly solutions revolutionized industries, emphasizing the symbiotic relationship between Analytical Intelligence and Creativity Intelligence.

Dikembe Mutombo, a former NBA star turned philanthropist, exemplifies the power of Interpersonal Intelligence and Emotional Resilience in life, success, and leadership. Through his humanitarian efforts, Mutombo exhibits an unwavering commitment to uplifting communities, showcasing how Emotional Intelligence and Ethical Intelligence can drive impactful social change. Bill Gates, a luminary in strategic foresight and business acumen, exemplifies the pivotal role of Analytical Intelligence and Practical Intelligence in life, success, and leadership. His capacity to envision the future and strategically navigate challenges underscores the indispensable nature of Holistic Intelligence.

Consider the story of Kip Thorne, a theoretical physicist who played a pivotal role in the discovery of gravitational waves. His ability to navigate ambiguity in the pursuit of groundbreaking discoveries exemplifies the fusion of Analytical Intelligence and Creativity Intelligence, setting an extraordinary example for those working in dynamic environments. Ai Weiwei, a Chinese artist and activist, exemplifies leadership through Creative Intelligence and Ethical Intelligence. His courage in challenging societal norms and fostering change highlights the transformative power of creativity combined with ethical discernment.

Intelligence, we argue, is a multidimensional tapestry that extends beyond the realms of EQ and IQ. The narrative expands to encompass luminaries like Michelle Obama, whose Emotional Resilience has been instrumental in navigating the complexities of public life; Winston Churchill's tenacity reflecting Emotional Resilience and Analytical Intelligence; Indra Nooyi's resourcefulness showcasing Practical Intelligence; Oprah Winfrey's self-belief embodying Intrapersonal Intelligence; Warren Buffett's analytical prowess highlighting Analytical Intelligence; Tim Cook's mindset shifting illustrating Cognitive and Emotional Flexibility; and Malala Yousafzai's challenge reframing, which integrates Ethical Intelligence and Emotional Resilience. These figures collectively weave a narrative that defies simplistic categorizations, embodying the holistic integration of multiple intelligences for impactful existence.

Our proposition revolves around the dynamic interplay of these diverse intelligences, each contributing uniquely to the tapestry of success. It is a paradigm that acknowledges the multifaceted strengths of individuals who excel not by adhering to a rigid framework but by skillfully navigating the intricate dance of the eight pillars of Holistic Intelligence. These exemplars, each embodying specific resilient characteristics, illustrate the power of a multidimensional approach to intelligence. The constellation of essential intelligences for triumphant existence encompasses ethical discernment, cultural acumen, creative ingenuity, relational adeptness, and more, forming a symphony that forges the crucible of true excellence.

This holistic fusion, a testament to the boundless potential of human intellect, breathes life into visionary endeavors, shaping the course of personal and professional journeys, and inspiring generations to come. In our journey to reimagine leadership and success, we must transcend the limiting paradigm of EQ versus IQ. Instead, let us embrace the Holistic Intelligence Model—a comprehensive framework that recognizes and celebrates the manifold facets of intelligence. Through this lens, we equip ourselves to tackle the complexities of modern life with nuance, wisdom, and unwavering determination, fostering a balanced and integrated approach to achieving unparalleled success.

Acknowledgements

Embarking on this journey of exploring the Holistic Intelligence Model and its application to leadership has been a profound experience, one that has been shaped by the guidance and support of numerous individuals. First and foremost, I extend my deepest gratitude to the Chief Officers of Fortune 100, 500, and 1000 companies who entrusted me with their most complex challenges. Your unwavering faith in my ability to devise solutions in seemingly impossible situations has been both humbling and empowering, providing real-world contexts in which the pillars of Emotional Resilience, Practical Intelligence, and Ethical Intelligence have been tested and refined.

I am indebted to the countless leaders I've had the privilege to work alongside throughout my career. Each interaction, each challenge faced together, has contributed to the insights and principles shared in this book. Your dedication to excellence, your unwavering commitment to your teams, and your willingness to embrace innovation have been a constant source of inspiration, highlighting the critical roles of Interpersonal Intelligence and Cultural Intelligence in effective leadership.

To my colleagues and mentors, both past and present, thank you for your invaluable guidance and wisdom. Your collective expertise and diverse perspectives have enriched my understanding of the eight pillars of Holistic Intelligence. It is through our collaborations that many of the concepts explored in these pages have taken shape, particularly in areas such as Analytical Intelligence and Creativity Intelligence, which have been instrumental in developing robust strategies for leadership and personal growth.

I extend a special thanks to those who have provided feedback and insights during the development of this book. Your thoughtful contributions have been instrumental in refining the ideas and ensuring their accessibility to a wide audience. Your willingness to engage in discussions, challenge assumptions, and share your own experiences has been invaluable in shaping the Ethical and Practical aspects of the Holistic Intelligence Model.

This book is a testament to the collective wisdom of leaders, past and present, who have left an indelible mark on the world. It is a tribute to the countless individuals who have demonstrated that leadership is not defined by titles, but by actions, by the impact we have on those we serve. It is a celebration of the potential that lies within each of us to lead with purpose, compassion, and a commitment to positive change, guided by the comprehensive framework of Holistic Intelligence.

Finally, to my family, whose unwavering support has been a constant source of strength, thank you for standing by my side throughout this endeavor. Your belief in me and in the importance of this work has been a driving force. This book is as much a reflection of your encouragement as it is of my own journey through the eight pillars of Holistic Intelligence.

With deepest gratitude,

William R. Stanek

Thriving Amidst Flux: Navigating Change and Uncertainty

Adapt. Lead. Flourish in a world of change.

Elevating Skills, Mindsets, and Strengths for Transformational Leadership in Your Personal and Professional Life

Includes a 2-week Action Plan for Leaders

William Stanek's Leadership Intelligence Mastery Series

William R. Stanek
Author & Series Creator

William Stanek's Leadership Intelligence Mastery Series

Elevating Skills, Mindsets, and Strengths for Transformational Leadership in Your Personal and Professional Life

Thriving Amidst Flux: Navigating Change and Uncertainty

Adapt. Lead. Flourish in a world of change.

Published by Stanek & Associates
in conjunction with
Big Blue Sky Press for Business
www.williamrstanek.com.

Copyright © 2025 William R. Stanek. Seattle, Washington. All rights reserved. Photographs of the author are © HC Stanek. Fine-art photographs and illustrations are © William R. Stanek and were created by the author.

No part of this book may be reproduced, stored in a retrieval system or transmitted in any form or by any means, electronic, mechanical, photocopying, recording, scanning or otherwise, except as permitted by Sections 107 or 108 of the 1976 United States Copyright Act, without the prior written permission of the publisher Requests to the publisher for permission should be sent to the address listed previously.

Stanek & Associates is a trademark of Stanek & Associates and/or its affiliates. All other marks are the property of their respective owners. No association with any real company, organization, person or other named element is intended or should be inferred through use of company names, web site addresses or screens.

This book expresses the views and opinions of the author. The information contained in this book is provided without any express, statutory or implied warranties.

LIMIT OF LIABILITY/DISCLAIMER OF WARRANTY: THE PUBLISHER AND THE AUTHOR MAKE NO REPRESENTATIONS OR WARRANTIES WITH RESPECT TO THE ACCURACY OR COMPLETENESS OF THE CONTENTS OF THIS WORK AND SPECIFICALLY DISCLAIM ALL WARRANTIES, INCLUDING WITHOUT LIMITATION WARRANTIES OF FITNESS FOR A PARTICULAR PURPOSE. NO WARRANTY MAY BE CREATED OR EXTENDD BY SALES OR PROMOTIONAL MATERIALS. THE ADVICE AND DISCUSSION IN THIS BOOK MAY NOT BE SUITABLE FOR EVERY SITUATION. THIS WORK IS SOLD WITH THE UNDERSTANDING THTAT THE PUBLISHER IS NOT ENGAGED IN RENDERING PROFESSIONAL SERVICES AND THAT SHOULD PROFESSIONAL ASSISTANCE BE REQUIRED THE SERVICES OF A COMPETENT PROFESSIONAL SHOULD BE SOUGHT. NEITHER THE PUBLISHERS, AUTHORS, RESELLERS NOR DISTRIBUTORS SHALL BE HELD LIABLE FOR ANY DAMAGES CAUSED OR ALLEGED TO BE CAUSE EITHER

DIRECTLY OR INDIRECTLY HEREFROM. THE REFERENCE OF AN ORGANIZATION OR WEBSITE AS A SOURCE OF FURTHER INFORMATION DOES NOT MEAN THAT THE PUBLISHER OR THE AUTHOR ENDORSES THE INFORMATION THE ORGANIZATION OR WEBSITE MAY PROVIDE OR THE RECOMMENDATIONS IT MAY MAKE. FURTHER, READERS SHOULD BE AWARE THAT WEBSITES LISTED IN THIS BOOK MAY NOT BE AVAILABLE OR MAY HAVE CHANGED SINCE THIS WORK WAS WRITTEN.

Stanek & Associates publishes in a variety of formats, including print, electronic and by print-on-demand. Some materials included with standard print editions may not be included in electronic or print-on-demand editions or vice versa.

Country of First Publication: United States of America.

Cover Design: Creative Designs Ltd.
Editorial Development: Andover Publishing Solutions
Content & Technical Review: L & L Technical Content Services

You can provide feedback related to this book by emailing the author at williamstanek @ aol.com. Please use the <u>name of the book</u> as the subject line.

1st Edition. Version: 1.0.1.0b

> **Note** I may periodically update this text and the edition and version number shown previously will let you know which version you are working with. If there's a specific feature you'd like me to write about in an update,

message me on Facebook (http://facebook.com/williamstanekauthor). Please keep in mind readership of this book determines how much time I can dedicate to it.

Special Notice for Groups and Teams Are you part of a group or team seeking comprehensive Empowered Leadership© and Inspirational Journeys© training? We offer tailored programs for groups of 12 or more, designed to equip you with the tools and strategies needed to thrive in today's dynamic landscape. Discover the power of collective growth and resilience! For inquiries and customized solutions, please reach out to Jeannie Kim jeannie.kim @ reagentpress.com.

Bulk Orders Available Looking to equip your team or organization with the transformative power of the "Leadership Intelligence Mastery" books? We offer special pricing and customized packages for bulk orders. For more information and to place your order, please contact Jeannie Kim jeannie.kim @ reagentpress.com.

Epigraph

In *The Resilient Leader*, we quoted Nelson Mandela:

> "The greatest glory in living lies not in never falling, but in rising every time we fall." - Nelson Mandela

You might be surprised to learn that Confucius expressed this same idea—more than 2,400 years earlier.

> "Our greatest glory is not in never falling, but in rising every time we fall." – Confucius

This striking parallel highlights the enduring nature of this wisdom. The belief that true strength lies not in avoiding failure but in rising after a fall transcends time, culture, and context. It's a universal truth that has been recognized and articulated by thinkers, philosophers, and leaders throughout history.

This shared understanding speaks to a profound truth about the human experience: resilience and perseverance are timeless virtues. They form the foundation for growth, leadership, and transformation, no matter the era or setting.

This timeless wisdom lies at the core of our exploration of emotional resilience and leadership excellence, serving as a reminder that the principles we study today are deeply rooted in the shared human journey.

Table of Contents

Note About the Front Matter 2
The Holistic Intelligence Model: The 8 Pillars of Personal and Professional Excellence 3
Letter from the Author 15
Our Foundational Proposition: Navigating the Complex Tapestry of Success 18
Acknowledgements 22
Epigraph 30
Table of Contents 31
Part 1. Let's Get Started! 39
    The 8 Pillars of Intelligence As a Framework for Transformative Leadership 40
    Opening Reflection 44
Charting Your Leadership Course 47
Thriving Amidst Flux 51
Thriving Amidst Flux: A 2-Week Action Plan 53
Instructions for the Action Plan 61
Thriving Amidst Flux: Navigating Change and Uncertainty in Dynamic Environments 67
Adaptability as a Leadership Competency 69
    The Importance of Adaptability in Leadership 69
    Key Components of Adaptability in Leadership 70
    Integrating Adaptability into Leadership Development 73
    Case Studies: Exemplary Adaptable Leaders 74
Understanding the Dynamics of Change 77

The Unparalleled Pace of Innovation 77
   Globalization and the Dissolution of Boundaries 78
   The Imperative for Proactive Leadership 79
   Embracing the Holistic Intelligence Model 79
   Case Study: Satya Nadella's Transformation of Microsoft .. 80
   The Consequences of Inertia 81
   Strategies for Comprehending and Leveraging Change 82
   Positioning for Sustained Success 82
   Looking Ahead 83

The Psychological Impact of Change on Individuals and Organizations 84
   Understanding Resistance to Change 84
   Strategies for Addressing Resistance 85
   Fostering Acceptance and Embracing Change 86
   Managing Change-Related Stress and Anxiety 87
   Integrating the Holistic Intelligence Model 89
   Case Study: Transforming Organizational Culture at IBM ... 90
   Practical Exercises and Tools 91
   Understanding Change Models 92
   Reflection Questions 93

Developing a Growth Mindset 95
   The Power of a Growth Mindset in Leadership 95
   Embracing Challenges as Opportunities 96
   Case Study: Netflix's Embrace of Innovation 97
   Cultivating a Learning-Oriented Perspective 98
   The Role of Feedback in Growth 99
   Case Study: Google's Culture of Learning 99

Integrating the Holistic Intelligence Model 100
Practical Strategies for Leaders 101
Overcoming Obstacles to a Growth Mindset 102
Reflection Questions... 102
Actionable Exercises... 103

Enhancing Cognitive Adaptability 106
Making Informed Decisions in Rapidly Changing Situations 106
Case Study: Johnson & Johnson's Tylenol Crisis 108
Leveraging Analytical Intelligence in Adapting to Change 109
Strategies to Enhance Analytical Intelligence 110
Balancing Analytical Intelligence with Other Intelligences 110
Case Study: Amazon's Data-Driven Culture 111
Practical Exercises to Enhance Cognitive Adaptability 111
Integrating the Holistic Intelligence Model 112
Reflection Questions... 113

Shifting from Reactive to Proactive Leadership 115
Anticipating Change and Preparing for Transition 115
Scenario Planning and Contingency Strategies 116
Embracing Change as an Opportunity 117
Case Study: Apple's Proactive Innovation 118
Fostering a Culture of Proactive Problem-Solving 118
Case Study: Toyota's Continuous Improvement Culture ... 120
Integrating the Holistic Intelligence Model 121
Practical Strategies for Leaders 122
Reflection Questions... 123

Actionable Exercises 124
Empowering and Supporting Your Team 126
   Providing Clear Communication and Guidance 126
   Case Study: Microsoft's Cultural Transformation................. 128
   Recognizing and Addressing Team Members' Concerns .. 129
   Case Study: Southwest Airlines' Employee-Centric Approach
   130
   Cultivating a Resilient Team Culture 131
   Integrating the Holistic Intelligence Model 132
   Practical Strategies and Exercises 133
   Reflection Questions 134
Leveraging Technology and Innovation 137
   Embracing Technological Solutions for Increased Agility . 137
   Strategies for Effective Technological Integration 140
   Case Study: General Electric's Digital Transformation 141
   Encouraging a Culture of Innovation and Experimentation
   142
   Case Study: 3M's Culture of Innovation 143
   Integrating the Holistic Intelligence Model 144
   Practical Strategies and Exercises 145
   Reflection Questions 148
Case Study 1: The Adaptable Leader in Action 151
   Background, Experience, and Leadership Style 151
   Key Situations Showcasing Adaptability 153
   Extracting Insights and Strategies 155
   Practical Takeaways for Leaders Navigating Change 156
Guided Self-Assessment: Evaluating Your Adaptability 158

Reflecting on Past Experiences with Change 158
Identifying Areas for Growth and Improvement 161
Overcoming Barriers to Adaptability 163
Strategies to Overcome Obstacles 163
Integrating the Holistic Intelligence Model 164
Action Plan Example 165
Practical Exercises and Tools 165
Reflection Questions 166
Embracing the Journey Toward Enhanced Adaptability 167

Setting Personalized Goals for Enhancing Adaptability 169
Defining Clear and Attainable Objectives 169
Introducing the WISE Framework for Goal-Setting 170
Components of the WISE Framework 170
Comparing WISE with SMART 172
Example of a WISE Goal 172
Implementing the WISE Framework 173
Benefits of the WISE Framework 174
Ready to Embrace the WISE Approach? 174
Identifying Key Areas for Development 175
Aligning Objectives with Personal Aspirations 175
Outlining Implementation Plans for Growth 176
Integrating the Holistic Intelligence Model 178
Practical Exercises and Tools 180
Reflection Questions 181
Case Study: Transforming Adaptability Through Goal Setting
.... 182
Embracing Continuous Growth 184

Case Study 2: The Adaptive Leader in Action 186
    Analyzing Key Instances Demonstrating Adapting to Change and Uncertainty in Leadership 189
    Extracting Insights and Strategies from the Case Study 192
    Lessons in Adapting to Change and Uncertainty from Antoine Girard's Leadership Style 200
    Practical Takeaways for Leaders Adapting to Change and Uncertainty 206

Leadership Case Reviews: Mastering Situations in Adapting to Change and Uncertainty 212

The Ongoing Journey of Adaptability in Leadership 218
    Embracing Change as a Catalyst for Growth 218
    Case Study: Netflix's Transformation 219
    Fostering a Culture of Innovation 220
    Creating an Environment Conducive to Experimentation. 221
    Case Study: 3M's Innovation Ecosystem 222
    Integrating the Holistic Intelligence Model 223
    Practical Strategies and Exercises 224
    Reflection Questions 225

Tools and Techniques for Adapting to Change and Uncertainty in Leadership 228
    1. Scenario Planning 228
    2. WISE Model 230
    3. Agile Methodologies 231
    4. Change Management Frameworks 232
    5. Technology Adoption 233
    6. Lean Thinking 235

7. Crisis Communication Strategies 236
  8. Stakeholder Engagement 237
  9. Innovation Labs and Incubators 239
  10. Adaptive Leadership Training 240
  11. Cross-Functional Teams 241
  12. Resilience Building Workshops 242
  13. Crisis Simulation Exercises 243
  14. Key Performance Indicators (KPIs) for Adaptability 245
  15. Customer Feedback Loops 246
  16. Networking and Industry Benchmarking 247
  17. Resource Allocation Models 248
  18. Futurist Thinking 249
  19. Cultivating an Adaptive Culture 250
  20. Strategic Alliances and Partnerships 251
  Integrating the Holistic Intelligence Model 252

Introducing GROW Analysis: A Comprehensive Framework for Strategic Development 255
  Components of GROW Analysis 255
  Implementing GROW Analysis 258
  Benefits of GROW Analysis 259
  GROW Analysis vs. SWOT Analysis 259
  Integrating GROW Analysis into Leadership Practices 260
  Ready to Implement GROW Analysis? 262
  Deep Dive: GROW Analysis 262

Fostering Adaptability in Your Team 267
  The Role of Leaders in Cultivating Team Adaptability 267
  Strategies to Promote Adaptability 268

Integrating the Holistic Intelligence Model 271

Practical Exercises for Developing Team Adaptability 272

Reflection Questions 274

Case Study: Fostering Adaptability at Adobe 275

Thoughtful Exploration: Thriving in Amidst Flux for Leaders **279**

About the Author: William R. Stanek **283**

Biography 284

Connect with William R. Stanek 285

Part 1. Let's Get Started!

Leadership Intelligence Mastery is a groundbreaking series that delves into the evolving landscape of leadership in the 21st century. It challenges the prevailing notion that Emotional Intelligence (EQ) and Intellectual Intelligence (IQ) alone suffice in the complex world of modern leadership. Instead, it introduces the Holistic Intelligence Model, a comprehensive framework that integrates eight essential pillars—Emotional Resilience (ER), Creativity Intelligence (CrQ), Practical Intelligence (PQ), Cultural Intelligence (CQ), Intrapersonal Intelligence (IntraQ), Interpersonal Intelligence (InterQ), Ethical Intelligence (EthQ), and Analytical Intelligence (AQ)—to redefine effective leadership.

In a rapidly changing global economy, leaders are tasked with navigating a myriad of challenges that demand more than traditional intelligence metrics. Leadership Intelligence Mastery recognizes that the divide between EQ and IQ is insufficient. By incorporating the eight pillars of the Holistic Intelligence Model, this series provides a robust framework that goes beyond conventional boundaries of intelligence. At its core, the books spotlight Emotional Resilience (ER) as the linchpin of effective leadership, equipping leaders to bounce back from setbacks, manage stress, and maintain a positive outlook even in the face of adversity.

Moreover, the series carefully dissects the distinctions between Emotional Resilience and EQ, emphasizing that ER transcends and encompasses emotional intelligence. It delves into the cognitive processes associated with understanding and managing emotions in high-pressure scenarios. By introducing the eight pillars of intelligence, including Creativity Intelligence (CQ) for driving innovation, Cultural Intelligence (CQ) for leading in a globalized world, and Ethical Intelligence (EthQ) for principled leadership, Leadership Intelligence Mastery offers a holistic approach that empowers leaders to thrive in every dimension of their roles.

The 8 Pillars of Intelligence As a Framework for Transformative Leadership

As a Framework for Transformative Leadership, the 8 Pillars of Intelligence represent a revolutionary approach, combining a diverse array of skills and perspectives that empower leaders to excel in today's dynamic environments. These pillars—Emotional Resilience (ER), Creativity Intelligence (CrQ), Practical Intelligence (PQ), Cultural Intelligence (CQ), Intrapersonal Intelligence (IntraQ), Interpersonal Intelligence (InterQ), Ethical Intelligence (EthQ), and Analytical Intelligence (AQ)—transcend traditional notions of intelligence, shaping leaders who are resilient, innovative, and impactful. Together, they form a foundation for a transformative leadership journey that is as practical as it is profound.

1. Emotional Resilience (ER): The Keystone of Leadership

Emotional Resilience is the core pillar that empowers leaders to remain composed under pressure, recover quickly from setbacks, and sustain a positive and focused outlook. It transcends traditional emotional intelligence, embodying a level of emotional fortitude that helps leaders face challenges with grace and inspire confidence in others.

2. Creativity Intelligence (CrQ): Driving Vision and Innovation

Creativity Intelligence equips leaders with the ability to think beyond boundaries, generate novel ideas, and adapt to change. This pillar is vital for problem-solving, fostering innovation, and guiding teams toward visionary solutions. Leaders with high CrQ turn challenges into opportunities for growth and transformation.

3. Practical Intelligence (PQ): Bridging Knowledge and Action

Practical Intelligence—sometimes referred to as "street smarts"—helps leaders effectively apply their knowledge to real-world situations. It emphasizes adaptability, resourcefulness, and sound decision-making in dynamic environments, ensuring that leadership strategies are actionable and results-oriented.

4. Cultural Intelligence (CQ): Leading in a Globalized World

Cultural Intelligence allows leaders to thrive in diverse and interconnected environments. By fostering a deep understanding of cultural norms, values, and practices, this pillar enables leaders to build authentic connections, foster inclusivity, and navigate cross-cultural dynamics with sensitivity and skill.

5. Intrapersonal Intelligence: Leading from Within

Intrapersonal Intelligence focuses on self-awareness and self-regulation, enabling leaders to understand their own emotions, motivations, and values. This pillar empowers leaders to align their actions with their purpose, making decisions rooted in authenticity and inspiring trust among their teams.

6. Interpersonal Intelligence: The Art of Influence and Connection

Interpersonal Intelligence helps leaders build meaningful relationships, foster collaboration, and navigate social dynamics effectively. With strong interpersonal skills, leaders can communicate clearly, resolve conflicts constructively, and create an environment of trust and mutual respect, driving team cohesion and shared purpose.

7. Ethical Intelligence (EthQ): Leadership with Integrity

Ethical Intelligence serves as the moral foundation for principled leadership. By upholding values such as honesty, accountability, and fairness, leaders with strong ethical intelligence make decisions that inspire trust, maintain credibility, and prioritize the greater good. This pillar is essential for building an ethical and sustainable leadership legacy.

8. Analytical Intelligence (AQ): Solving Complexity with Clarity

Analytical Intelligence equips leaders with critical thinking and problem-solving skills needed to make sound, evidence-based decisions. By discerning patterns, evaluating risks, and analyzing data, leaders with strong analytical intelligence navigate complexity with precision and deliver effective, strategic outcomes.

A Symphony of Interconnected Intelligences

Embracing the Holistic Intelligence Model means embarking on a transformative journey where each pillar contributes uniquely to your leadership narrative. Whether you are stepping into a new leadership role, facing unprecedented challenges, or seeking to enhance your personal growth, the eight pillars provide a comprehensive roadmap to guide your path. Integrate Emotional Resilience (ER) to maintain composure and inspire your team during turbulent times, leverage Creativity Intelligence (CrQ) to drive innovation and strategic vision, and apply Practical Intelligence (PQ) to translate ideas into actionable plans. Enhance your leadership effectiveness by cultivating Cultural Intelligence (CQ) to navigate globalized environments, Intrapersonal Intelligence (IntraQ) for self-awareness and authentic decision-making, Interpersonal Intelligence (InterQ) to build strong, collaborative relationships, Ethical Intelligence (EthQ) to uphold integrity and trust, and Analytical Intelligence (AQ) to solve complex problems with clarity and precision.

Together, these pillars form a symphony of intelligences that empower you to lead with resilience, creativity, practicality, cultural sensitivity, self-awareness, interpersonal adeptness, ethical integrity, and analytical prowess. As you integrate these facets into your leadership practice, you will not only excel in your roles but also inspire those around you to achieve their fullest potential, creating a legacy of impactful and sustainable leadership.

Opening Reflection

Before you continue, take a moment to center yourself with the photograph that follows.

As you gaze upon this Hawaiian horizon, where the sun meets the sea, envision your leadership journey stretching out before you. Like the rhythmic crash of waves against the rocky shoreline, your path may be marked by challenges, yet it is also adorned with moments of beauty and triumph. Just as the sun dips below the horizon, signaling the close of one day and the promise of another, your journey in leadership is a series of endings and beginnings. Embrace them all, for they are the threads that weave the tapestry of your growth and resilience.

The interplay of light and shadow in this Hawaiian sky mirrors the dynamic nature of leadership. Each experience, each decision, shapes your narrative, much like the shifting colors of the sky influence the mood of the moment. With each step, you etch your unique story into the sands of time, drawing upon the eight pillars of the Holistic Intelligence Model—from Emotional Resilience (ER) that provides strength during tumultuous times to Creativity Intelligence (CQ) that sparks innovative solutions. Let the spirit of the islands infuse your path with vitality and inspiration, empowering you to lead with purpose, passion, and resilience.

In this moment, on this shore, you stand at the threshold of a transformative journey. Let the timeless beauty of this photograph serve as a beacon, guiding you back to the essence of your leadership journey. Just as the boardwalk stretches ahead, disappearing into the horizon, your leadership odyssey is filled with boundless opportunities and unforeseen turns. Embrace each step with curiosity and purpose, knowing that every challenge met and every triumph celebrated is a testament to your strength and resilience. Embrace the path, for it is uniquely yours to shape, guided by the comprehensive framework of the Holistic Intelligence Model.

And if ever the winds of uncertainty threaten to steer you off course, return to this photograph. Let the timeless beauty of this moment serve as a beacon, guiding you back to the essence of your leadership journey. Remember, every challenge met, every triumph celebrated, is a testament to your strength and resilience. Embrace the path, for it is uniquely yours to shape.

When faced with crossroads, remember this mountain road. It symbolizes the choices, the uncharted territories, and the possibilities that await. As you stand at the precipice of decisions, know that each step, even the uncertain ones, contributes to your leadership odyssey. Embrace the journey, for every turn leads to growth, to wisdom, to your unique legacy. Keep forging ahead, for the road not taken is the one that defines your extraordinary story.

Charting Your Leadership Course

My journey through the intricacies of leadership has unfolded amidst some of the most pivotal moments in modern history. From the tense era of the Cold War to the turbulent times of the Iraq War, I found myself navigating through significant conflicts that tested our nation's resilience. What distinguishes me is my exceptional ability not only to adapt but to thrive in these high-pressure environments. Time and again, I was thrust into senior leadership positions, defying my relatively junior rank. This speaks volumes about my knack for evaluating critical situations and skillfully guiding those around me—often individuals significantly senior to me—toward resounding success, grounded in the eight pillars of the Holistic Intelligence Model.

My experiences, shaped in the crucible of the military and other arenas, have granted me profound insights: genuine leadership surpasses mere titles or years of service. It revolves around the ability to inspire and influence, to steer a team through even the most daunting challenges. In my role as a technology consultant, I often assumed the mantle of the "fixer" – the one summoned when situations seemed dire and hope was fading. Surprisingly, I discovered that more often than not, the root cause of many seemingly insurmountable problems was not a technological failure but rather a breakdown in leadership and intelligence dynamics. This realization reinforced the importance of Emotional Resilience

(ER), Interpersonal Intelligence (InterQ), and Analytical Intelligence (AQ) in effective leadership.

Recognizing this recurring pattern, my consulting focus naturally evolved toward uncovering people-centric solutions. It became evident that the success of any endeavor, particularly in the fast-paced and constantly evolving landscape of technology, hinges on the human element. This revelation forms the foundation of the principles expounded in our book, emphasizing that effective leadership is a multifaceted endeavor encompassing Emotional Resilience (ER), Practical Intelligence (PQ), Ethical Intelligence (EthQ), and the other pillars of holistic intelligence. By delving into the human dynamics that underpin every facet of professional life, our book provides a comprehensive guide for individuals looking to excel in their roles and lead with authenticity, empathy, and strategic acumen. Through a series of exercises, case studies, reflective practices, and more, readers will gain invaluable insights into honing their own intelligences, fostering a deeper understanding of themselves and those they lead.

Ultimately, this book is a testament to the idea that true leadership is a holistic endeavor, requiring a keen awareness of oneself, an astute understanding of others, and an unwavering commitment to ethical and principled decision-making. It's a call to action for leaders at every level and in every industry to embrace the complexities of human dynamics and harness them as a force for positive change and lasting success. Together, let us embark on this journey of reimagining leadership intelligence, shaping a future where leadership transcends convention and inspires profound transformation.

As you step into this transformative phase, remember that every milestone, every challenge, and every triumph is a thread woven into the tapestry of your leadership journey. Embrace each moment with curiosity and purpose, for it is through this journey that you will discover the true depth of your leadership potential. Let the Holistic Intelligence Model guide you, ensuring that your leadership is resilient, innovative, ethical, and profoundly impactful.

Let your gaze linger on the boardwalk that stretches ahead, disappearing into the horizon. Much like this path, your leadership journey unfurls before you, an odyssey filled with boundless opportunities and unforeseen turns. The distant pagoda-like structure beckons, a symbol of your destination, a testament to your aspirations.

Embrace the ebb and flow, for just as the tides shape the estuary, experiences shape leadership. The interplay of shadows and light in the sky above mirrors the dynamic nature of challenges and triumphs you'll encounter. Each step is a stitch in the fabric of your leadership narrative, weaving together resilience, wisdom, and growth.

With every footfall, you write your own story of leadership. As you traverse this boardwalk, know that you carry with you the potential to create profound impact. The journey itself is your canvas, waiting for the brush strokes of your unique vision. Embrace it with an open heart and a steadfast spirit, for the path you walk is yours to shape and yours to own.

Thriving Amidst Flux

Thriving Amidst Flux: A 2-Week Action Plan

Embarking on the journey to enhance your adaptability as a leader requires intentional effort and structured guidance. This 2-week action plan is designed to help both aspiring leaders and seasoned professionals grasp, apply, and integrate the principles outlined in our book. The plan offers a balanced mix of reading, reflection, practical exercises, and application of tools and techniques, all while providing the flexibility to tailor it to your specific needs and aspirations.

Week 1: Building a Foundation

Day 1: Introduction and Orientation

- **Objective:** Familiarize yourself with the action plan and set intentions for the upcoming two weeks.
- **Time Allocation:** 1-2 hours
- **Action:**
- Review the Table of Contents and understand the structure of the book.
- Read The Holistic Intelligence Model, Letter From the Author and Our Foundational Proposition to understand the unique approach of the book.
- Set personal goals for what you aim to achieve through this action plan.
- Begin a Gratitude Journal to cultivate a positive mindset (15 minutes).

Day 2: Understanding Adaptability in Leadership

- **Objective:** Grasp the fundamental concepts of adaptability as a leadership competency.

- **Time Allocation:** 2-3 hours
- **Action:**
- Read the Let's Get Started, Charting Your Leadership Course and Adaptability as a Leadership Competency sections.
- Summarize key points and reflect on how adaptability impacts leadership effectiveness.
- Journal your initial thoughts and insights (Daily Journaling, 15 minutes).

Day 3: Reflecting on Past Experiences with Change

- **Objective:** Gain self-awareness by analyzing your previous encounters with change.
- **Time Allocation:** 2-3 hours
- **Action:**
- Engage with the Guided Self-Assessment section.
- Complete the Reflecting on Past Experiences with Change exercise.
- Identify patterns and themes in your responses to change.
- Journal your reflections and insights (Reflection Journaling, 15 minutes).

Day 4: Identifying Areas for Growth and Improvement

- **Objective:** Pinpoint specific aspects of adaptability to develop further.
- **Time Allocation:** 2-3 hours
- **Action:**
- Continue with the Guided Self-Assessment.
- Complete the Identifying Areas for Growth and Improvement exercise.
- Set initial personal development goals based on your self-assessment.

- Update your journal with identified growth areas and aspirations.

Day 5: Introduction to Adaptability Tools and Techniques
- **Objective:** Familiarize yourself with various tools and techniques to enhance adaptability.
- **Time Allocation:** 2-3 hours
- **Action**:
- Read the Tools and Techniques for Adapting to Change and Uncertainty in Leadership section.
- Highlight tools that resonate most with your current needs.
- Reflect on how these tools can be applied in your leadership role.
- Journal your thoughts and plan which tools to focus on during Week 2.

Day 6: Exploring Case Study 1: The Adaptable Leader in Action
- **Objective:** Learn from real-life examples of adaptable leadership.
- **Time Allocation:** 1.5 – 2.5 hours
- **Action:**
- Read and analyze Case Study 1: The Adaptable Leader in Action.
- Extract key strategies and lessons learned.
- Reflect on how these strategies can be integrated into your leadership approach.
- Journal your reflections and action points.

Day 7: Weekly Reflection and Consolidation

- **Objective:** Review and consolidate the learnings from Week 1.
- **Time Allocation:** 1.5 – 2 hours
- **Action:**
- Revisit your journal entries from the week.
- Summarize the key insights and progress made.
- Adjust your personal development goals if necessary.
- Celebrate your achievements and set intentions for Week 2.

Week 2: Applying Tools, Techniques, and Fostering Team Adaptability

Day 8: Setting Personalized Goals for Enhancing Adaptability

- **Objective:** Define clear, WISE goals to guide your adaptability journey.
- **Time Allocation:** 2-3 hours
- **Action:**
- Read the Setting Personalized Goals for Enhancing Adaptability section.
- Use the Goal-Setting Worksheet to define your WISE goals.
- Outline an Action Plan for each goal, including steps, resources, and timelines.
- Journal your goals and action plans.

Day 9: Implementing Scenario Planning

- **Objective:** Develop foresight and prepare for various future scenarios.
- Time Allocation: 2-4 hours
- **Action:**

- Dive into the tools that most resonated with you from the Tools and Techniques section, such as Scenario Planning.
- Conduct a Scenario Planning Workshop using a real or hypothetical change relevant to your organization.
- Document the scenarios and corresponding action plans.
- Reflect on the exercise and journal your learnings.

Day 10: Engaging with Case Study 2: The Adaptive Leader in Action

- **Objective:** Gain deeper insights from another real-life adaptable leader.
- **Time Allocation:** 1.5 – 2.5 hours
- **Action:**
- Read and analyze Case Study 2: The Adaptive Leader in Action.
- Identify the adaptive strategies employed and their outcomes.
- Compare and contrast with Case Study 1.
- Journal your reflections and consider how to apply these strategies.

Day 11: Applying Methodologies in Leadership

- **Objective:** Enhance team flexibility and responsiveness through practices discussed in the Tools and Techniques section.
- **Time Allocation:** 2-3 hours
- **Action:**
- Study the Tools and Techniques section.
- Implement related project or practice, such as a small Agile project or practice Scrum/Kanban techniques with your team.

- Monitor progress and gather feedback.
- Journal your experiences and insights.

Day 12: Fostering a Culture of Innovation in Your Team
- **Objective:** Cultivate an environment that encourages creativity and experimentation.
- **Time Allocation:** 2-3 hours
- **Action:**
- Read the Encouraging a Culture of Innovation and Experimentation and the Fostering a Culture of Innovation sections.
- Identify and implement at least two strategies to promote innovation within your team.
- **Examples:** Host a brainstorming session, establish an innovation lab, or launch an idea management system.
- Encourage team members to share and experiment with new ideas.
- Journal the outcomes and team feedback.

Day 13: Utilizing the GROW Analysis Framework
- **Objective:** Apply structured approaches to manage organizational transitions effectively.
- **Time Allocation:** 2-3 hours
- **Action:**
- Explore the Introducing GROW Analysis section.
- Develop a plan for an upcoming or ongoing change initiative.
- Assign roles and responsibilities based on the GROW components.
- Journal your plan and anticipate potential challenges.

Day 14: Reflection, Self-Assessment, and Forward Planning

- **Objective:** Evaluate your progress and plan for continued growth in adaptability.
- **Time Allocation:** 2-3 hours
- **Action:**
- Complete a Final Self-Assessment to measure your adaptability growth over the two weeks.
- Reflect on the exercises, case studies, and tools applied.
- Identify areas of strength and opportunities for further development.
- Update your Personal Development Plan with new goals and action steps.
- Celebrate your progress and set intentions for ongoing adaptability enhancement.

To support your journey through this action plan, consider leveraging the following tools and resources:

- **Journaling Apps:** Tools like Day One, Evernote, or Microsoft OneNote to document your reflections, insights, and progress.
- **Mindfulness Apps:** Applications such as Headspace, Calm, or Insight Timer for guided meditation and mindfulness exercises.
- **Goal-Setting Worksheets:** Templates to define and track your personal development goals, available on platforms like Canva or Google Docs.
- **Books by William Stanek:** Dive deeper into leadership and personal development by exploring the Leadership Intelligence Mastery Library by William Stanek. These books

provide invaluable insights and practical strategies to enhance your growth and understanding.
- **Resilience Workshops:** Participate in or organize workshops focused on building emotional resilience and adaptive thinking.

Adaptability is a cornerstone of effective leadership in today's dynamic world. By following this 2-week action plan, you will not only enhance your own adaptability but also empower your team to navigate change with confidence and creativity. Embrace this journey with an open mind, commitment, and the willingness to continuously learn and grow. As you integrate these principles into your leadership practice, you'll be well-equipped to lead your organization toward sustained success amidst the ever-present flux of the modern business environment.

Instructions for the Action Plan

The action plan offers a structured approach to integrate the strategies discussed in this book into your leadership style, whether you're starting your leadership journey or looking to enhance your existing leadership skills.

While the action plan is initially structured as a two-week schedule, it's important to note that both the schedule and all other aspects of the plan can be fully customized to align with your individual needs and preferences:

- **Personalization**   Tailor the suggested activities to align with your current level of leadership experience, preferences, and specific leadership context.

- **Allocate Flexible Time**   Recognize that the suggested schedule and time allocations are flexible. Adjust them to accommodate your availability and preferences. Focus on quality engagement rather than rigid adherence to schedules and time frames.

- **Reflect and Internalize**   After completing each session or activity, take time to reflect on the insights gained. Internalize how they can be applied to your unique leadership challenges and opportunities.

As an added component, contemplate including the following optional activities as part of the action plan:

- **Discussion Forums**   Engage with fellow leaders in discussions related to the content. Share experiences, insights, and challenges for mutual learning. This platform caters to leaders at various stages of their careers.

- **Weekly Q&A Sessions**   Attend live Q&A sessions to seek clarifications, share progress, and gain additional guidance from peers and experts. These sessions are beneficial for both aspiring leaders and experienced professionals looking to exchange insights.

- **Resource Library**   Explore the supplementary materials provided to deepen your understanding and application of resilience concepts. This resource is valuable regardless of your level of leadership experience.

Here are some overarching tips to assist you on your journey:

- **Consistency is Key**   Engage consistently with the material and activities to embed resilience practices into your leadership style, regardless of your current leadership level.

- **Balance Learning and Application**   Strike a balance between learning from the book and actively applying the concepts in your leadership role. This approach is beneficial for leaders at all stages.

- **Document Progress**   Keep a journal to record your reflections, insights, and challenges. Track your growth in resilience over time. This practice is valuable for leaders at any point in their journey.

- **Seek Feedback**   Encourage open communication with your team or peers. Seek feedback on your leadership style and adjust your approach based on their input. This applies to leaders at any stage of their careers.

- **Stay Open-Minded** Embrace new ideas and perspectives. Be open to adapting your leadership style based on the insights gained. This attitude is crucial for leaders at all levels.

- **Celebrate Milestones** Acknowledge and celebrate your achievements, no matter how small. Recognize your growth in resilience. This practice is relevant for leaders at any stage of their careers.

By following the structured action plan, you will not only gain a deeper understanding but also develop practical skills. The journey towards transformative leadership is ongoing, and each step you take contributes to your continued growth and development, regardless of your level of experience.

For aspiring leaders when the action plans suggest applying concepts to your leadership role, keep the following in mind:

- **Understand the Concept** Begin by thoroughly understanding the concept or principle outlined in the action plan. Take time to grasp its significance and how it contributes to effective leadership.

- **Reflect on Relevance** Consider how this concept applies to your current leadership aspirations and goals. Reflect on specific situations or scenarios where you can implement this principle.

- **Identify Opportunities** Even if you haven't held formal leadership positions yet, there are likely opportunities within your academic, professional, or personal life where you can exhibit leadership qualities. Look for chances to take initiative, influence others positively, or demonstrate resilience.

- **Experiment and Practice**   Apply the concept in these identified opportunities. Experiment with different approaches and observe the outcomes. Pay attention to what works well and what may require adjustments.

- **Seek Feedback**   Don't hesitate to ask for feedback from mentors, supervisors, or peers who have experience in leadership roles. Their insights can provide valuable guidance on how you can further develop and apply these leadership skills.

- **Reflect on Learnings**   After applying the concept, take time to reflect on the experience. Consider what went well, what challenges you faced, and what you learned from the process.

- **Document Achievements**   Keep a record of instances where you successfully applied the concept. This documentation serves as tangible evidence of your developing leadership abilities and can be valuable when discussing your leadership potential in future endeavors.

- **Continuously Learn and Adapt**   Aspire to be a lifelong learner. Stay open to new ideas and seek opportunities for growth. Adapt your approach based on the insights gained from applying leadership concepts.

Leadership is not solely defined by titles or formal positions. As an aspiring leader, you have the capacity to demonstrate leadership qualities in various capacities. Embrace these opportunities to cultivate and showcase your leadership potential. Each step you take now lays the foundation for your future leadership journey.

Lastly, whether you're an aspiring leader or an experienced one, keep the following points in mind:

- **Consistency and Patience**   Developing leadership skills is a journey that requires consistency and patience. It's important to acknowledge that growth takes time, and each step forward, no matter how small, is a valuable progression.

- **Adaptability**   Leadership is a dynamic field, and the ability to adapt to changing circumstances and environments is crucial. Remain open to new ideas, feedback, and emerging trends in leadership.

- **Leverage Networks**   Building a network of mentors, peers, and industry contacts can provide valuable insights and opportunities for growth. Don't hesitate to seek advice or engage in discussions with others who have experience in leadership.

- **Embrace Failure**   Failure is a natural part of the learning process. It's important to view setbacks as opportunities for growth and learning. Embrace challenges, learn from mistakes, and use them as stepping stones toward future success.

- **Self-Care and Well-Being**   Effective leadership starts with taking care of oneself. Prioritize physical, emotional, and mental well-being to ensure you have the energy and resilience needed to lead effectively.

- **Setting Personal Goals** Consider setting specific, measurable goals related to your leadership development. These goals can provide a clear direction for your journey and serve as milestones to track your progress.

- **Seek Additional Resources** Beyond the book, there are numerous resources available to support leadership development. This may include workshops, courses, seminars, and industry-specific publications. Stay curious and explore these opportunities.

- **Reflection and Continuous Improvement** Regularly take time to reflect on your leadership journey. Consider what has been effective, areas for improvement, and the direction you want to take in your leadership development.

- **Celebrate Achievements** Acknowledge and celebrate your achievements, no matter how small. Recognizing your progress can boost confidence and motivation, reinforcing your commitment to leadership growth.

- **Stay Inspired** Find sources of inspiration that resonate with you. Whether it's books, TED talks, podcasts, or biographies of influential leaders, seek out content that fuels your passion for leadership.

Leadership is a multifaceted skill that evolves over time. Embrace the process, stay committed to your growth, and remain open to new experiences and knowledge. The journey toward becoming an effective leader is not only professionally fulfilling but also personally enriching.

Thriving Amidst Flux: Navigating Change and Uncertainty in Dynamic Environments

- "Leadership is not merely about steering the ship through calm waters, but about charting a course through the storms with vision and resilience."

In the dynamic landscape of modern leadership, adaptability is crucial. Here, we focus on navigating change and uncertainty in environments that demand quick thinking and nimble responses. We explore strategies and principles that empower leaders not only to weather storms of uncertainty but to thrive amidst them, ensuring their teams and organizations remain agile and effective.

In the dynamic landscape of modern business, change and uncertainty have become constants rather than exceptions. Technological advancements, globalization, and rapidly evolving market trends shape the way organizations operate. To navigate this ever-shifting terrain, leaders must possess a crucial competency: adaptability. This book delves into the art and science of thriving amidst change and uncertainty, exploring the foundational principles of adaptability and offering actionable strategies for leaders seeking to excel in dynamic environments.

As the pace of change continues to accelerate, leaders find themselves in a perpetual state of transition. The ability to not only weather change but to harness it as a force for innovation and growth distinguishes exceptional leaders. By understanding the psychological impact of change, fostering a growth mindset, and building resilience, leaders can lay the groundwork for success in an unpredictable world.

Through real-world examples and practical insights, this book also highlights the experiences of an adaptable leader, showcasing how effective decision-making and resilience in the face of rapid change can drive organizational success. From proactive leadership techniques to leveraging technology and innovation, this section offers a comprehensive toolkit for leaders to not only navigate change but to lead through it.

We encourage self-reflection and personal growth. By assessing one's own adaptability and setting tailored goals for development, leaders can embark on a journey towards heightened agility and effectiveness. Embracing change as a catalyst for growth and innovation is not only a leadership skill; it is a mindset that paves the way for sustained success in today's fast-paced business world. Join us as we explore the essential strategies for thriving in dynamic environments and mastering the art of adaptability in leadership.

Adaptability as a Leadership Competency

- "Adaptability is the hallmark of exceptional leadership; it empowers leaders to navigate complexities with grace and inspire their teams to excel."

In today's fast-paced and ever-changing business landscape, adaptability has emerged as a critical competency for effective leadership. The ability to navigate uncertainty, embrace change, and inspire others to do the same is no longer optional—it's essential. This section explores the significance of adaptability as a core leadership competency, delving into its impact on organizational success and outlining strategies for leaders to develop and embody this vital trait.

The Importance of Adaptability in Leadership

Leaders are constantly faced with new challenges, from technological advancements and market disruptions to shifting customer expectations and global events. Adaptability enables leaders to:

- **Respond Swiftly to Change:** Quickly adjust strategies and operations in response to emerging trends.
- **Innovate Continuously:** Foster a culture of innovation that keeps the organization competitive.
- **Mitigate Risks:** Anticipate potential issues and develop contingency plans.
- **Seize Opportunities:** Recognize and capitalize on new possibilities for growth.

Adaptable leaders contribute to the resilience of their organizations by:

- **Modeling Flexibility:** Demonstrating openness to new ideas and approaches.
- **Empowering Teams:** Encouraging team members to take initiative and embrace change.
- **Driving Engagement:** Cultivating an environment where employees feel valued and motivated.
- **Building Trust:** Establishing credibility through consistent and transparent actions.

Research indicates that organizations led by adaptable leaders often experience:

- **Higher Employee Satisfaction:** Teams feel supported and are more engaged.
- **Improved Innovation Rates:** A culture of adaptability fosters creative problem-solving.
- **Better Financial Performance:** Agile organizations can pivot quickly to meet market demands.
- **Sustained Competitive Advantage:** The ability to adapt becomes a differentiator in the marketplace.

Key Components of Adaptability in Leadership

1. Emotional Resilience

Definition: The capacity to manage emotions effectively, remain composed under pressure, and recover quickly from setbacks.

Importance in Leadership:
- **Stability:** Provides a steadying influence during times of uncertainty.
- **Decision-Making:** Enables clear thinking when faced with complex challenges.
- **Team Morale:** Positively influences the emotional climate of the team.

Development Strategies:
- **Mindfulness Practices:** Engage in meditation or reflective exercises.
- **Stress Management Techniques:** Incorporate physical activity, relaxation methods, or hobbies.
- **Support Networks:** Seek mentorship or peer support.

2. Cognitive Flexibility

Definition: The ability to shift thinking strategies, consider multiple perspectives, and adapt mental processes to new situations.

Importance in Leadership:
- **Problem-Solving:** Facilitates innovative solutions to complex issues.
- **Learning Agility:** Promotes continuous learning and adaptability.
- **Strategic Thinking:** Enhances the ability to anticipate and plan for future scenarios.

Development Strategies:
- **Expose to Diverse Experiences:** Engage with different cultures, industries, or disciplines.

- **Challenge Assumptions:** Regularly question existing beliefs and consider alternatives.
- **Lifelong Learning:** Pursue education and professional development opportunities.

3. Learning Agility

Definition: The willingness and ability to learn from experiences and apply that learning to perform successfully in new situations.

Importance in Leadership:
- **Adaptation:** Quickly assimilate new information and skills.
- **Growth Mindset:** Encourage a culture of continuous improvement.
- **Performance Enhancement:** Apply lessons learned to improve outcomes.

Development Strategies:
- **Reflective Practices:** Regularly assess experiences to extract insights.
- **Seek Feedback:** Actively solicit input from others to identify growth areas.
- **Embrace Challenges:** View new tasks as opportunities to learn.

4. Decision-Making Under Uncertainty

Definition: The ability to make informed decisions without having complete information, balancing risk and opportunity.

Importance in Leadership:

- **Timeliness:** Make prompt decisions to keep pace with change.
- **Confidence:** Inspire trust through decisive action.
- **Risk Management:** Evaluate potential outcomes to minimize negative impacts.

Development Strategies:

- **Scenario Analysis:** Practice making decisions in hypothetical situations.
- **Data Utilization:** Use available data to inform choices, recognizing limitations.
- **Collaborative Decision-Making:** Involve others to gain diverse insights.

Integrating Adaptability into Leadership Development

Self-Assessment Tools

- **Feedback:** Gather input from peers, subordinates, and supervisors to understand adaptability strengths and areas for improvement.
- **Personality Assessments:** Use tools like William Stanek's Resilient Growth Self-Assessment and the 8 Pillars of Leadership: Self-Assessment to gain self-awareness.
- **Adaptability Quotient (AQ) Assessments:** Evaluate your ability to adjust to new conditions and learn from experiences.

Training and Development Programs

- **Workshops and Seminars:** Attend sessions focused on change management, resilience, and innovation.

- **Online Courses:** Utilize platforms like Coursera, LinkedIn Learning, or Harvard Business School Online for flexible learning.
- **Executive Education:** Enroll in leadership development programs offered by universities or professional organizations.

Coaching and Mentoring

- **Professional Coaching:** Engage with executive coaches specializing in adaptability and leadership.
- **Mentorship Relationships:** Seek guidance from experienced leaders who exemplify adaptability.
- **Peer Learning Groups:** Join forums or mastermind groups to share experiences and learn collaboratively.

Case Studies: Exemplary Adaptable Leaders

Case Study 1: Satya Nadella – CEO of Microsoft

Background:

Situation: Upon becoming CEO in 2014, Nadella faced a stagnating Microsoft with declining relevance in the mobile and cloud computing markets.

Adaptability in Action:

Cultural Transformation: Shifted Microsoft's culture from a "know-it-all" to a "learn-it-all" mindset.

Embracing Cloud Computing: Pivoted the company's focus to cloud services with Azure.

Open Innovation: Encouraged collaboration, including partnerships with competitors.

Outcomes:

Revitalized Growth: Microsoft regained its position as a leading technology company.

Increased Market Value: The company's market capitalization surpassed $1 trillion.

Enhanced Employee Engagement: Improved morale and a more innovative culture.

Case Study 2: Indra Nooyi – Former CEO of PepsiCo

Background:

Situation: Faced with changing consumer preferences toward healthier options.

Adaptability in Action:

Strategic Shift: Implemented "Performance with Purpose" to focus on healthier products.

Portfolio Diversification: Expanded offerings to include nutritious options.

Sustainability Initiatives: Integrated environmental and social considerations into business strategy.

Outcomes:

Revenue Growth: Increased revenues through new product lines.

Brand Reputation: Strengthened PepsiCo's image as a socially responsible company.

Industry Influence: Set new standards for corporate responsibility.

Understanding the Dynamics of Change

In the modern business arena, change is no longer an intermittent visitor but a constant companion. It is a relentless force propelling organizations toward new possibilities and challenges. Today's business landscape is shaped by intricate dynamics, where the rate of innovation is not just rapid but exponential. Leaders are compelled to not only keep pace with these changes but to anticipate and leverage them for strategic advantage.

The Unparalleled Pace of Innovation

Technological advancements have become the heartbeat of this relentless change. Breakthroughs in artificial intelligence, machine learning, blockchain, and quantum computing are not just altering existing industries—they are birthing entirely new ones. These technologies disrupt traditional business models, redefine customer expectations, and demand a fundamental rethinking of strategies and operations.

- **Artificial Intelligence and Machine Learning:** AI and ML are transforming data analytics, customer service, and operational efficiency. Businesses that harness these technologies can gain unprecedented insights and automate complex processes, outpacing competitors who lag in adoption.
- **Blockchain Technology:** Beyond cryptocurrencies, blockchain offers secure and transparent transaction

records, revolutionizing supply chain management, financial services, and even voting systems.

- **Quantum Computing:** Although in its nascent stages, quantum computing promises to solve problems currently beyond the reach of classical computers, potentially disrupting cybersecurity, pharmaceuticals, and material sciences.

Leaders must recognize that understanding and integrating these technologies is not optional. It is a strategic imperative that determines organizational relevance and survival in the digital age.

Globalization and the Dissolution of Boundaries

Globalization has woven a complex tapestry of interconnected markets and cultures. Boundaries that once defined markets are dissolving, leading to a hyper-competitive global landscape.

- **Interconnected Economies:** Economic shifts in one region can have ripple effects worldwide. Supply chain disruptions, trade policies, and international relations now play pivotal roles in business strategy.
- **Cultural Diversity and Inclusion:** With global operations, businesses must navigate diverse cultural norms and values. Cultural intelligence becomes essential for leaders to manage international teams, negotiate with global partners, and market effectively across different regions.
- **Regulatory Complexity:** Operating globally means complying with a multitude of regulatory frameworks. Leaders must be adept at understanding international laws,

trade agreements, and compliance standards to avoid legal pitfalls and capitalize on global opportunities.

The Imperative for Proactive Leadership

In this ever-accelerating environment, reactive leadership is insufficient. Leaders must adopt a proactive stance, characterized by foresight, agility, and a willingness to embrace change.

- **Anticipating Trends:** By staying ahead of industry trends and technological advancements, leaders can position their organizations to capitalize on emerging opportunities before competitors.
- **Cultivating Innovation:** Fostering a culture that encourages experimentation and values creative thinking allows organizations to adapt quickly and innovate continuously.
- **Strategic Agility:** Agile leaders can pivot strategies in response to market shifts, ensuring organizational resilience. This involves flexible planning, rapid decision-making, and empowering teams to act decisively.

Embracing the Holistic Intelligence Model

The challenges of navigating change underscore the importance of the Holistic Intelligence Model's 8 Pillars:

1. **Emotional Resilience (ER):** Leaders must manage stress and remain steadfast in the face of uncertainty, providing stability for their teams.
2. **Creativity Intelligence (CrQ):** Innovative thinking enables leaders to devise novel solutions to complex problems, a necessity in uncharted territories.

3. **Practical Intelligence (PQ):** Applying knowledge effectively ensures that strategic initiatives are grounded in reality and can be executed successfully.
4. **Cultural Intelligence (CQ):** Navigating global markets requires an understanding and appreciation of cultural nuances, fostering better relationships and collaborations.
5. **Intrapersonal Intelligence:** Self-awareness allows leaders to recognize their strengths and limitations, facilitating personal growth and authentic leadership.
6. **Interpersonal Intelligence:** Building strong relationships and effective communication channels is vital for team cohesion and stakeholder engagement.
7. **Ethical Intelligence (EthQ):** Maintaining integrity and ethical standards builds trust, a critical asset in times of change.
8. **Analytical Intelligence (AQ):** Data-driven decision-making helps leaders assess risks and opportunities with greater precision.

Case Study: Satya Nadella's Transformation of Microsoft

Satya Nadella's leadership at Microsoft exemplifies thriving amidst flux. Upon becoming CEO in 2014, Nadella recognized the need for cultural and strategic overhaul. He shifted Microsoft's focus to cloud computing and AI, embracing open-source initiatives and fostering a growth mindset within the organization.

- **Cultural Shift:** Nadella emphasized empathy, collaboration, and learning, breaking down silos and encouraging innovation.
- **Technological Adoption:** Under his guidance, Microsoft became a leader in cloud services with Azure, adapting to changing market demands.
- **Strategic Partnerships:** He forged alliances with former competitors, expanding Microsoft's ecosystem and global reach.

Nadella's approach, aligning with the 8 Pillars, demonstrates how leaders can navigate change effectively by integrating emotional intelligence, cultural awareness, and strategic agility.

The Consequences of Inertia

Failing to adapt to the dynamics of change can have dire consequences. Organizations that resist transformation risk obsolescence.

- **Kodak's Decline:** Once a titan of photography, Kodak's reluctance to embrace digital technology led to its downfall. Despite inventing the first digital camera, the company feared cannibalizing its film business, allowing competitors to dominate the digital market.
- **Blockbuster vs. Netflix:** Blockbuster's failure to innovate and adapt to the streaming revolution paved the way for Netflix to reshape the entertainment industry.

These examples underscore the critical need for leaders to champion change rather than resist it.

Strategies for Comprehending and Leveraging Change

Continuous Learning:

- Professional Development: Encourage leaders and employees to engage in lifelong learning to stay abreast of industry developments.
- Knowledge Sharing: Create platforms for sharing insights and experiences within the organization.

Environmental Scanning:

- Market Analysis: Regularly assess market trends, customer behaviors, and competitor strategies.
- Technological Vigilance: Monitor emerging technologies that could disrupt or enhance business operations.

Stakeholder Engagement:

- Customer Feedback: Actively seek input from customers to understand their evolving needs and expectations.
- Employee Involvement: Involve team members at all levels in strategy discussions to gain diverse perspectives.

Scenario Planning:

- Risk Assessment: Identify potential risks associated with change and develop mitigation strategies.
- Opportunity Mapping: Explore various future scenarios to prepare for different outcomes.

Positioning for Sustained Success

By comprehending the forces driving transformation, leaders can craft strategies that not only respond to change but leverage it to create competitive advantages.

- **Adaptive Strategy Development:** Regularly revisit and adjust strategic plans to align with the changing environment.
- **Investment in Innovation:** Allocate resources to research and development, fostering an environment where new ideas can flourish.
- **Building Resilient Cultures:** Cultivate organizational cultures that are flexible, inclusive, and resilient, enabling swift adaptation to new challenges.

Looking Ahead

As we proceed, the focus will shift to practical methodologies and mindsets essential for mastering change. Leaders will be equipped with tools to foster innovation, build agile teams, and develop foresight.

- **Fostering Cultures of Innovation:** Strategies for encouraging creativity and risk-taking within teams.
- **Agile Leadership Practices:** Techniques for increasing responsiveness and flexibility in leadership approaches.
- **Developing Strategic Foresight:** Methods for anticipating future trends and preparing the organization accordingly.

Understanding the dynamics of change is the first step in a leader's journey toward thriving in dynamic environments. By embracing change as an integral component of the business landscape and leveraging the principles of the Holistic Intelligence Model, leaders can navigate uncertainties with confidence and guide their organizations toward sustained success.

The Psychological Impact of Change on Individuals and Organizations

Change is an inherent part of growth and progress, yet it often brings with it a whirlwind of emotions and reactions. For both individuals and organizations, change can stir a complex psychological landscape that leaders must navigate with empathy and strategic insight. This section delves into the intricate psychological dimensions accompanying change, illuminating the spectrum from resistance to acceptance, and offering valuable strategies to manage the stress and anxiety associated with transitions.

Understanding Resistance to Change

Human beings have an innate preference for the familiar and predictable. This inclination toward the status quo arises from a fundamental need for stability, security, and control. When confronted with change, individuals may experience fear of the unknown, loss of control, or concern over their ability to adapt. Resistance to change can manifest in various ways:

- **Passive Resistance:** Subtle behaviors such as procrastination, decreased productivity, or reluctance to engage.
- **Active Resistance:** Overt opposition, vocal criticism, or attempts to undermine change initiatives.
- **Emotional Responses:** Feelings of anxiety, frustration, confusion, or resentment.

Factors Contributing to Resistance:

- **Fear of the Unknown:** Uncertainty about future roles, responsibilities, or job security.
- **Loss of Control:** Perceived threat to autonomy or influence within the organization.
- **Comfort with Current State:** Satisfaction with existing processes and skepticism about the need for change.
- **Lack of Trust:** Doubts about leadership motives or past experiences with unsuccessful changes.
- **Inadequate Communication:** Insufficient information leading to misunderstandings or rumors.

Strategies for Addressing Resistance

Effective leadership involves recognizing and proactively addressing resistance:

1. Open and Transparent Communication:

- Provide Clear Information: Explain the reasons for change, expected benefits, and potential challenges.
- Two-Way Dialogue: Encourage questions and feedback to clarify misunderstandings and involve employees in the conversation.

2. Empathy and Support:

- Acknowledge Emotions: Validate feelings and show understanding of the concerns employees may have.
- Offer Support Resources: Provide training, counseling, or mentorship programs to ease the transition.

3. Involvement and Participation:

- Engage Employees: Involve team members in planning and implementation to foster ownership and reduce resistance.
- Empower Decision-Making: Allow employees to contribute ideas and have input on how changes are executed.

4. Demonstrate Leadership Commitment:

- Lead by Example: Show commitment to change through actions and attitudes.
- Consistency: Ensure that messages and behaviors align to build credibility and trust.

5. Highlight Quick Wins:

- Early Successes: Showcase immediate benefits or improvements resulting from the change to build momentum and confidence.

Fostering Acceptance and Embracing Change

Acceptance represents a positive shift where individuals recognize the inevitability of change and its potential advantages. Leaders can cultivate acceptance by:

1. Creating a Compelling Vision:

- Articulate Future Goals: Paint a clear and inspiring picture of what the organization aims to achieve.
- Align Personal and Organizational Goals: Show how change benefits both the company and employees' personal development.

2. Building Trust and Credibility:

- Consistency in Actions and Words: Follow through on promises and maintain integrity.

- Transparency: Be honest about challenges and uncertainties, fostering an environment of trust.

3. Recognizing and Rewarding Adaptability:
- Acknowledge Efforts: Celebrate those who contribute positively to change initiatives.
- Provide Incentives: Offer rewards or opportunities for professional growth tied to embracing change.

4. Cultivating a Growth Mindset:
- Encourage Learning: Promote continuous development and view setbacks as opportunities for growth.
- Support Innovation: Create a safe space for experimentation and creative problem-solving.

Managing Change-Related Stress and Anxiety

Change can trigger stress and anxiety due to uncertainties and perceived threats to one's well-being. The effects can be significant:

- **Physical Symptoms:** Headaches, fatigue, sleep disturbances, or illness.
- **Emotional Symptoms:** Irritability, mood swings, feelings of overwhelm.
- **Cognitive Symptoms:** Difficulty concentrating, indecision, negative thinking.
- **Behavioral Symptoms:** Withdrawal from social interactions, increased absenteeism, decreased performance.

Emotional resilience, the first pillar of the Holistic Intelligence Model, is critical in managing stress and adapting to change. It enables individuals to:

- **Adapt to New Situations:** Adjust to changes with a positive attitude.
- **Maintain Emotional Balance:** Regulate emotions in the face of stress.
- **Recover from Setbacks:** Bounce back from difficulties and learn from experiences.

Strategies for Managing Stress and Anxiety

1. Promote Psychological Safety:

- Create an Open Environment: Encourage open dialogue without fear of judgment or reprisal.
- Listen Actively: Show genuine interest in employees' thoughts and feelings.

2. Provide Support and Resources:

- Access to Professional Help: Offer employee assistance programs, counseling, or mental health services.
- Training and Development: Equip employees with skills to handle new responsibilities or technologies.

3. Encourage Self-Care Practices:

- Work-Life Balance: Promote reasonable work hours and time off.
- Wellness Programs: Implement initiatives that focus on physical health, such as fitness classes or healthy eating options.
- Effective Communication:

- Regular Updates: Keep employees informed to reduce uncertainty.
- Clarity and Consistency: Provide clear messages to prevent confusion.

4. Model Resilient Behavior:

- Demonstrate Composure: Show steadiness in challenging times.
- Share Coping Strategies: Discuss personal methods for managing stress.

5. Foster Social Support:

- Team Building Activities: Strengthen relationships and collaboration.
- Peer Support Networks: Encourage mentorship and buddy systems.

Integrating the Holistic Intelligence Model

The psychological impact of change underscores the need for leaders to develop and apply multiple intelligences:

- **Emotional Resilience (ER):** Managing personal stress and guiding others through emotional challenges.
- **Intrapersonal Intelligence:** Self-awareness to recognize and regulate one's own emotional responses.
- **Interpersonal Intelligence:** Building strong relationships and effective communication to support others.
- **Ethical Intelligence (EthQ):** Making principled decisions that consider the well-being of employees.
- **Cultural Intelligence (CQ):** Understanding diverse perspectives and how they influence reactions to change.

- **Analytical Intelligence (AQ):** Assessing situations accurately to inform strategic responses.

Case Study: Transforming Organizational Culture at IBM

Background:

In the early 1990s, IBM faced significant challenges due to market shifts and internal inefficiencies. Lou Gerstner was appointed CEO to turn the company around.

Challenges:

Employee Resistance: Long-standing employees were accustomed to a hierarchical and risk-averse culture.

Market Competition: Rapid technological changes required agile responses.

Leadership Actions:

1. Cultural Shift:
- **Breaking Silos:** Encouraged collaboration across departments.
- **Customer Focus:** Redirected emphasis from internal processes to customer needs.

2. Open Communication:
- **Transparent Messaging:** Gerstner communicated openly about the company's challenges and the necessity for change.
- **Employee Engagement:** Held town halls and encouraged feedback.

3. Empowering Employees:
- **Decision-Making Authority:** Delegated more responsibility to frontline employees.
- **Recognition Programs:** Acknowledged and rewarded adaptability and innovation.

Outcomes:
- **Renewed Growth:** IBM reinvented itself, focusing on services and solutions rather than just hardware.
- **Employee Buy-In:** By addressing resistance and managing stress, employees became advocates for change.

Practical Exercises and Tools

Exercise 1: Change Readiness Assessment

1. Self-Reflection:
- **Assess Personal Attitude:** Reflect on your own feelings toward change.
- **Identify Triggers:** Recognize what aspects of change cause stress or resistance.

2. Team Assessment:
- **Survey Employees:** Gather feedback on their concerns and readiness.
- **Identify Support Needs:** Determine what resources or support would help ease the transition.

Exercise 2: Developing a Communication Plan

1. Key Messages:
- **Define Core Information:** What do employees need to know?

- **Craft Clear Messages:** Ensure clarity and relevance.

2. Channels and Frequency:
- **Select Appropriate Mediums:** Email, meetings, intranet, etc.
- **Establish Regular Updates:** Set a consistent schedule for communication.

3. Feedback Mechanisms:
- **Provide Platforms for Input:** Suggestion boxes, Q&A sessions.
- **Respond Promptly:** Acknowledge and address concerns raised.

Understanding Change Models

1. Kubler-Ross Change Curve:
- **Stages:** Denial, Anger, Bargaining, Depression, Acceptance.
- **Application:** Recognize where individuals are on the curve to tailor support.

2. ADKAR Model:
- **Awareness:** Understanding the need for change.
- **Desire:** Motivation to participate and support change.
- **Knowledge:** How to change.
- **Ability:** Implementing new skills and behaviors.
- **Reinforcement:** Sustaining change.

Research Findings

Statistics on Change Failure:

- **70% of Change Initiatives Fail:** Often due to employee resistance and lack of management support (McKinsey & Company).

Impact of Stress on Productivity:

- **Decreased Performance:** High stress levels can reduce productivity by up to 60% (American Institute of Stress).

Reflection Questions

1. Personal Experience:

- How do you typically react to change?
- What strategies have helped you cope with change in the past?

2. Leadership Approach:

- How can you apply emotional resilience to support your team?
- What steps can you take to improve communication during transitions?

3. Organizational Culture:

- What aspects of your organization's culture support or hinder change?
- How can you contribute to fostering a more adaptable environment?

—

Recognizing and addressing the psychological impact of change is a cornerstone of effective leadership in dynamic environments. By understanding the roots of resistance and employing strategies to foster acceptance, leaders can ease transitions and enhance organizational resilience. Managing change-related stress and anxiety not only supports individual well-being but also contributes to sustained performance and a positive organizational culture.

Leaders who navigate the emotional terrain of change with empathy, clear communication, and strategic support pave the way for a smoother journey through transformation. Embracing the principles of the Holistic Intelligence Model equips leaders with the tools to guide their teams successfully, turning the challenges of change into opportunities for growth and innovation.

Developing a Growth Mindset

In an era defined by rapid change and uncertainty, cultivating a growth mindset is one of the most potent tools at a leader's disposal. Coined by psychologist Carol S. Dweck, a growth mindset refers to the belief that abilities and intelligence can be developed through dedication, hard work, and perseverance. This contrasts with a fixed mindset, where individuals see their talents and abilities as static traits. Embracing a growth mindset empowers leaders and their teams to navigate challenges, innovate, and continuously improve, laying the groundwork for a resilient and adaptable organization.

The Power of a Growth Mindset in Leadership

Leaders with a growth mindset view challenges not as threats but as opportunities to learn and grow. This perspective fosters resilience, adaptability, and a proactive approach to problem-solving. By modeling and promoting a growth mindset, leaders can:

- **Enhance Individual and Team Performance:** Encouraging continuous learning leads to skill development and increased competence.
- **Foster Innovation:** An open attitude toward experimentation and learning from failures drives creative solutions.

- **Build Resilience:** Viewing setbacks as learning experiences strengthens the ability to bounce back from adversity.
- **Cultivate a Positive Organizational Culture:** A growth-oriented environment attracts talent and promotes employee engagement.

Embracing Challenges as Opportunities

A growth mindset begins with reframing how we perceive obstacles. Instead of seeing challenges as insurmountable barriers, individuals with a growth mindset interpret them as:

- **Learning Opportunities:** Each challenge provides valuable lessons that contribute to personal and professional growth.
- **Catalysts for Development:** Overcoming difficulties strengthens skills and builds confidence.
- **Stepping Stones to Success:** Setbacks are viewed as temporary and necessary steps on the path to achievement.

Strategies for Leaders:

1. Model Growth Mindset Behaviors:

- Share Personal Experiences: Discuss times when you faced challenges and how you grew from them.
- Demonstrate Openness: Show willingness to tackle difficult tasks and embrace new experiences.

2. Promote a Positive Attitude Toward Challenges:

- Encourage Risk-Taking: Support team members in stepping out of their comfort zones.
- Normalize Failure: Emphasize that failures are a natural part of the learning process.

3. Set Stretch Goals:
- Challenge Your Team: Assign tasks that require effort beyond current capabilities.
- Provide Support: Offer resources and guidance to help achieve these goals.

Case Study: Netflix's Embrace of Innovation

Background:

Netflix, originally a DVD rental service, faced a significant challenge with the advent of streaming technology and changing consumer preferences.

Growth Mindset in Action:
- **Innovation Over Comfort:** Instead of clinging to their successful DVD model, Netflix embraced streaming technology, recognizing the opportunity for growth.
- **Continuous Learning:** The company invested heavily in understanding digital distribution and consumer behavior.
- **Risk-Taking Culture:** Netflix encourages experimentation, even if it leads to failures, fostering an environment where new ideas are welcomed.

Outcome:

Netflix transformed into a global leader in streaming services, continually adapting to market changes and setting industry standards.

Cultivating a Learning-Oriented Perspective

Central to a growth mindset is the belief that learning is an ongoing journey. Leaders can cultivate this perspective by:

- **Encouraging Curiosity:** Promote questioning and exploration of new ideas.
- **Providing Learning Opportunities:** Offer training, workshops, and access to educational resources.
- **Recognizing Effort and Improvement:** Acknowledge progress and the pursuit of knowledge, not just end results.

Strategies for Leaders:

1. Create a Culture of Continuous Improvement:

- **Implement Learning Programs:** Establish regular training sessions and development programs.
- **Support Professional Development:** Encourage attendance at conferences, courses, and seminars.

2. Facilitate Knowledge Sharing:

- **Cross-Functional Teams:** Promote collaboration across different departments to broaden perspectives.
- **Mentorship Programs:** Pair experienced employees with those looking to develop specific skills.

3. Encourage Reflective Practices:

- **Regular Feedback Sessions:** Provide constructive feedback and encourage self-assessment.
- **After-Action Reviews:** Analyze projects to identify lessons learned and areas for improvement.

The Role of Feedback in Growth

Feedback is a critical component of a learning-oriented environment. It provides insights into performance and areas for development.

- **Constructive Feedback:** Focus on specific behaviors and outcomes, offering actionable suggestions.
- **Open Dialogue:** Encourage two-way communication where team members can also provide feedback to leaders.
- **Timely Responses:** Provide feedback promptly to reinforce learning when experiences are fresh.

Implementing Effective Feedback Mechanisms:

- **Feedback:** Collect input from peers, subordinates, and supervisors for a comprehensive view.
- **Regular Check-Ins:** Schedule consistent one-on-one meetings to discuss progress and challenges.
- **Feedback Training:** Teach employees how to give and receive feedback constructively.

Popular feedback models include 360-Degree Feedback, the Feedforward Approach and the Holistic Feedback System (HFS) developed by William Stanek.

Case Study: Google's Culture of Learning

Background:

Google is renowned for its innovative culture and emphasis on learning and development.

Growth Mindset in Action:

- **20% Time Policy:** Employees are encouraged to spend 20% of their time on projects they are passionate about, fostering creativity and learning.
- **Access to Resources:** Google offers extensive internal training programs and resources for skill development.
- **Emphasis on Data and Feedback:** Decisions are data-driven, and employees are encouraged to learn from outcomes.

Outcome:

This culture has led to groundbreaking products like Gmail and Google Maps, originated from employees' innovative projects.

Integrating the Holistic Intelligence Model

Developing a growth mindset aligns closely with several pillars of the Holistic Intelligence Model:

- **Emotional Resilience (ER):** A growth mindset enhances resilience by reframing setbacks as learning opportunities.
- **Creative Intelligence (CrQ):** Embracing challenges stimulates creative thinking and problem-solving.
- **Intrapersonal Intelligence:** Self-awareness and self-regulation are key in recognizing fixed mindset tendencies and shifting perspectives.
- **Interpersonal Intelligence:** Promoting a learning culture strengthens relationships through shared growth experiences.

- **Analytical Intelligence (AQ):** Continuous learning improves critical thinking and the ability to analyze complex situations.

Practical Strategies for Leaders

Self-Assessment and Mindset Shift

1. Reflect on Your Mindset:

- **Identify Fixed Mindset Triggers:** Recognize situations where you may avoid challenges or feel threatened by others' success.
- **Challenge Limiting Beliefs:** Replace thoughts like "I can't do this" with "I can't do this yet."

2. Set Personal Development Goals:

- **Commit to Learning:** Identify areas where you want to grow and set specific objectives.
- **Seek Feedback:** Ask for input from peers and mentors to gain new perspectives.

Building a Growth Mindset in Teams

1. Communicate the Value of Growth:

- **Share Success Stories:** Highlight examples where embracing challenges led to positive outcomes.
- **Articulate Benefits:** Explain how a growth mindset contributes to personal fulfillment and organizational success.

2. Encourage Experimentation:

- **Safe Environment for Risks:** Allow room for failure without punitive consequences.

- **Reward Innovation:** Recognize creative solutions and efforts to improve.

3. Provide Resources and Support:
- **Access to Training:** Offer courses and workshops relevant to employees' roles and interests.
- **Mentorship and Coaching:** Facilitate relationships that support learning and development.

Overcoming Obstacles to a Growth Mindset

Addressing Fixed Mindset Behaviors
- **Perfectionism:** Encourage focusing on progress over perfection.
- **Fear of Failure:** Normalize failure as part of the learning process.
- **Comparison with Others:** Emphasize personal growth rather than competition.

Dealing with Organizational Barriers
- **Hierarchical Structures:** Promote open communication and flatten hierarchies where possible.
- **Resistance to Change:** Address underlying fears and provide clear rationales for change initiatives.
- **Lack of Psychological Safety:** Build trust through transparency and consistent support.

Reflection Questions

1. Personal Mindset:
- When faced with a significant challenge, do you see it as an opportunity or a threat? Why?

- How do you react to feedback or criticism? Do you use it to grow or feel discouraged?

2. Leadership Practices:
- What steps can you take to model a growth mindset for your team?
- How can you create an environment where team members feel safe to take risks and learn from mistakes?

3. Organizational Culture:
- Does your organization's culture support continuous learning? Why or why not?
- What changes can be implemented to promote a growth mindset across the organization?

Actionable Exercises

Exercise 1: Growth Mindset Journaling
- **Daily Reflection:** At the end of each day, write about a challenge you faced and what you learned from it.
- **Identify Patterns:** Look for recurring themes in your responses to challenges.
- **Set Intentions:** Determine how you will apply these lessons moving forward.

Exercise 2: Learning Goals Setting
- **Skills Inventory:** List skills you wish to develop or improve.
- **Create a Plan:** For each skill, outline steps to acquire or enhance it, including resources and timelines.
- **Monitor Progress:** Regularly review and adjust your plan as needed.

Exercise 3: Team Learning Workshops
- **Organize Knowledge-Sharing Sessions:** Team members present on topics of interest or recent learnings.
- **Collaborative Projects:** Form cross-functional teams to work on innovative solutions.
- **Feedback Rounds:** Practice giving and receiving feedback in a structured, supportive setting.

Developing a growth mindset is a cornerstone of building emotional resilience and adaptability in the face of change and uncertainty. By embracing challenges as opportunities and fostering a learning-oriented perspective, leaders can transform the way they and their teams perceive and respond to obstacles. This shift not only enhances individual capabilities but also cultivates a culture of continuous improvement and innovation.

Leaders who prioritize the growth mindset principles pave the way for their organizations to thrive in dynamic environments. They unlock the potential of their teams, drive performance, and position their organizations to navigate the complexities of the modern business landscape successfully.

Additional Insights

Research Findings
- **Impact on Performance:** Studies by American Psychologist Carol Dweck and her colleagues have shown that organizations fostering a growth mindset culture have

employees who are more committed, innovative, and willing to go the extra mile.
- **Neuroplasticity Evidence:** Neuroscience supports the growth mindset, demonstrating that the brain continues to develop and change throughout life in response to learning and experience.

Quotes to Inspire

Carol Dweck: "Becoming is better than being."

Nelson Mandela: "I never lose. I either win or learn."

Thomas Edison: "I have not failed. I've just found 10,000 ways that won't work."

Enhancing Cognitive Adaptability

- "True adaptability begins in the mind; by embracing diverse perspectives, we expand our capacity to navigate the ever-changing tides of leadership."

In an era characterized by rapid technological advancements, shifting market dynamics, and unprecedented global events, leaders must develop a heightened capacity for cognitive adaptability. Cognitive adaptability refers to the mental agility to adjust one's thinking and decision-making processes in response to changing circumstances. It is a crucial component of effective leadership in dynamic environments.

Let's explore the critical skills and strategies required to make informed decisions in rapidly changing situations and delve into the role of analytical intelligence—a key pillar of the Holistic Intelligence Model—in effectively adapting to change.

Making Informed Decisions in Rapidly Changing Situations

Cognitive flexibility is the mental ability to switch between thinking about two different concepts or to think about multiple concepts simultaneously. For leaders, this means being able to shift perspectives, adapt strategies, and consider alternative solutions quickly.

Key Principles for Effective Decision-Making

1. Maintain a Clear and Focused Mindset

- **Emotional Regulation:** High-pressure situations can trigger stress responses that cloud judgment. Practicing mindfulness and stress management techniques can help leaders remain calm and focused.
- **Pause and Reflect:** Even when time is limited, taking a brief moment to assess the situation can prevent impulsive decisions.
- **Prioritize Objectives:** Clarify what is most important in the moment to focus efforts effectively.

2. Gather and Assess Relevant Information

- **Situational Awareness:** Stay attuned to both internal and external factors affecting the organization.
- **Ask the Right Questions:** Identify what information is critical and seek it out proactively.
- **Leverage Networks:** Utilize expertise within and outside the organization to gain diverse perspectives.

3. Embrace Agility in Thinking

- **Scenario Planning:** Consider multiple potential outcomes and develop contingency plans.
- **Adaptability:** Be willing to pivot strategies as new information emerges.
- **Innovative Problem-Solving:** Encourage creative approaches to challenges.

Strategies to Enhance Decision-Making Skills

Develop Decision-Making Frameworks:

- **GROW Analysis (Gains, Realities, Opportunities, Weaknesses):** Assess internal and external factors systematically.
- **Decision Trees:** Visualize possible choices and their potential consequences.
- **Cost-Benefit Analysis:** Weigh the pros and cons quantitatively and qualitatively.

Foster a Decision-Supportive Environment:

- **Empower Teams:** Delegate authority to make decisions at appropriate levels, accelerating response times.
- **Promote Open Communication:** Encourage team members to share insights and raise concerns without fear.
- **Establish Clear Protocols:** Define processes for decision-making during crises to reduce ambiguity.

Case Study: Johnson & Johnson's Tylenol Crisis

In 1982, Johnson & Johnson faced a crisis when tampered Tylenol capsules led to customer deaths. The company's swift and decisive actions are a hallmark of effective decision-making under pressure.

- **Maintained Focused Mindset:** Leadership prioritized customer safety over short-term financial loss.
- **Gathered Information:** Quickly assembled facts and consulted experts.
- **Made Decisive Actions:** Issued a nationwide recall, demonstrating commitment to consumer well-being.

- **Leveraged Analytical Intelligence:** Assessed the situation thoroughly to rebuild trust and implement tamper-proof packaging.

Leveraging Analytical Intelligence in Adapting to Change

Analytical Intelligence (AQ), one of the 8 Pillars of the Holistic Intelligence Model, is crucial for leaders to navigate complex challenges. It encompasses critical thinking, logical reasoning, and the ability to analyze data to make evidence-based decisions.

The Role of Analytical Intelligence

1. Evaluating Complex Situations

- **Data Interpretation:** Analyze quantitative and qualitative data to understand trends and patterns.
- **Problem Identification:** Accurately pinpoint the root causes of issues rather than just addressing symptoms.
- **Risk Assessment:** Evaluate potential risks and uncertainties to inform strategic choices.

2. Anticipating Trends and Future Developments

- **Predictive Analysis:** Use data analytics and modeling to forecast future scenarios.
- **Market Intelligence:** Monitor industry developments, competitor actions, and consumer behaviors.
- **Technological Awareness:** Stay informed about emerging technologies that could impact the organization.

3. Informed Decision-Making

- **Evidence-Based Approach:** Rely on factual information and empirical evidence rather than assumptions.
- **Balanced Judgment:** Combine analytical insights with intuition and experience.
- **Continuous Learning:** Update knowledge bases regularly to keep analyses relevant.

Strategies to Enhance Analytical Intelligence

1. Invest in Data Literacy

- **Training and Development:** Provide education on data analysis tools and methodologies.
- **Promote Analytical Thinking:** Encourage questioning and critical evaluation of information.

2. Implement Data-Driven Practices

- **Utilize Business Intelligence Tools:** Leverage software for data visualization and real-time analytics.
- **Establish Metrics and KPIs:** Define clear performance indicators to measure progress and outcomes.

3. Foster Collaborative Analysis

- **Cross-Functional Teams:** Bring together diverse expertise to enhance problem-solving capabilities.
- **Knowledge Sharing:** Create platforms for sharing insights and best practices within the organization.

Balancing Analytical Intelligence with Other Intelligences

While analytical intelligence provides a robust foundation for decision-making, it should be complemented by:

- **Emotional Intelligence (EQ):** Understanding the human element, such as employee morale and customer sentiments.
- **Practical Intelligence (PQ):** Drawing on experience and instinct when data is incomplete or ambiguous.
- **Ethical Intelligence (EthQ):** Ensuring decisions align with ethical standards and organizational values.

Case Study: Amazon's Data-Driven Culture

Amazon's success is largely attributed to its data-driven decision-making culture.

- **Customer-Centric Approach:** Uses data analytics to understand customer preferences and tailor experiences.
- **Innovation through Analytics:** Employs predictive analytics to optimize supply chain management and logistics.
- **Balancing Data with Innovation:** Encourages experimentation (e.g., Amazon Web Services) while grounding decisions in data.

Practical Exercises to Enhance Cognitive Adaptability

Exercise 1: Scenario Analysis Workshop
- **Objective:** Improve ability to anticipate and respond to various future scenarios.
- **Steps:**
- 1. Identify a key challenge facing the organization.
- 2. Develop multiple potential future scenarios (best case, worst case, most likely).

- 3. For each scenario, outline possible responses and strategies.
- **Outcome:** Enhanced readiness and flexible thinking.

Exercise 2: Critical Thinking Drills

- **Objective:** Strengthen analytical reasoning and problem-solving skills.
- **Steps:**
- 1. Present a complex problem without an obvious solution.
- 2. Encourage team members to ask probing questions.
- 3. Analyze information critically to arrive at potential solutions.
- **Outcome:** Improved ability to dissect problems and consider multiple angles.

Exercise 3: Data Interpretation Sessions

- **Objective:** Boost data literacy and confidence in handling data.
- **Steps:**
- 1. Provide datasets relevant to the business.
- 2. Practice interpreting data, identifying trends, and drawing conclusions.
- 3. Discuss findings and implications for decision-making.
- **Outcome:** Enhanced ability to leverage data effectively.

Integrating the Holistic Intelligence Model

Enhancing cognitive adaptability involves developing multiple intelligences:

- **Analytical Intelligence (AQ):** Core to evaluating information and making informed decisions.

- **Emotional Resilience (ER):** Helps maintain clarity under pressure.
- **Creative Intelligence (CrQ):** Encourages innovative thinking when standard solutions are insufficient.
- **Practical Intelligence (PQ):** Ensures that decisions are actionable and grounded in reality.
- **Intrapersonal Intelligence:** Self-awareness to recognize cognitive biases and limitations.
- **Interpersonal Intelligence:** Facilitates collaboration and effective communication during decision-making processes.

Reflection Questions

1. Self-Assessment:
- How do you typically approach decision-making in high-pressure situations?
- What steps do you take to ensure your decisions are informed and objective?

2. Analytical Skills:
- Are there areas where your data literacy could be improved?
- How do you balance data analysis with intuition in your decision-making process?

3. Team Development:
- How can you foster a culture that values analytical thinking and data-driven decisions?
- What resources or training could support your team's cognitive adaptability?

Enhancing cognitive adaptability is essential for leaders aiming to navigate the complexities of rapid change effectively. By cultivating the ability to make informed decisions swiftly and leveraging analytical intelligence, leaders can position their organizations to respond proactively to evolving challenges.

Developing these skills requires a commitment to continuous learning, self-awareness, and the integration of multiple intelligences. Leaders must foster environments that encourage critical thinking, data literacy, and collaborative problem-solving.

In embracing both the quantitative rigor of analytical intelligence and the qualitative insights from emotional and practical intelligences, leaders can achieve a holistic approach to decision-making. This balance ensures that decisions are not only data-informed but also considerate of human factors and ethical implications.

By enhancing cognitive adaptability, leaders empower themselves and their teams to not only survive but thrive amid relentless change, turning uncertainty into opportunities for innovation and growth.

Shifting from Reactive to Proactive Leadership

- "A proactive leader does not wait for change to happen, but anticipates the winds of transformation and sets the sails accordingly."

In the ever-evolving landscape of modern business, leaders must transcend a reactive stance and embrace a proactive approach to navigate change effectively. Reactive leadership—responding to events after they occur—can leave organizations perpetually playing catch-up, often at a significant disadvantage. In contrast, proactive leadership anticipates challenges and opportunities, positioning organizations to navigate change with confidence and agility.

This section illuminates the critical aspects of proactive leadership, including anticipating change, preparing for transitions, and fostering a culture of proactive problem-solving. By shifting from a reactive to a proactive mindset, leaders can empower their organizations to not only adapt to change but to shape it, driving innovation and sustained success.

Anticipating Change and Preparing for Transition

Proactive leaders are adept at anticipating change before it occurs, allowing them to prepare and strategize for smooth transitions. This involves developing foresight—the ability to predict or plan for the future by analyzing current trends and potential disruptions. Leaders cultivate foresight through:

- **Environmental Scanning:** Regularly monitoring external factors such as market trends, technological advancements, regulatory changes, and socio-economic shifts.
- **Trend Analysis:** Identifying patterns over time to forecast future developments.
- **Stakeholder Engagement:** Gathering insights from customers, employees, suppliers, and industry experts to understand emerging needs and challenges.

By cultivating a forward-thinking perspective, leaders can position their organizations to adapt swiftly and seize opportunities presented by change.

Scenario Planning and Contingency Strategies

One key strategy for anticipating change is scenario planning. This involves envisioning various future scenarios and developing contingency plans for each. By considering a range of potential outcomes—optimistic, pessimistic, and most likely—leaders can ensure that their organizations are prepared to navigate change, regardless of its nature or magnitude.

Steps in Scenario Planning:
- **1. Identify Driving Forces:** Determine the key factors that will influence the future of the organization, such as technological trends, market dynamics, and competitive actions.

- **2. Develop Scenarios:** Create detailed narratives for each potential future scenario, outlining how these driving forces could interact.
- **3. Assess Impacts:** Analyze how each scenario would affect the organization's operations, finances, and strategic objectives.
- **4. Formulate Strategies:** Develop plans to respond effectively to each scenario, including actions to mitigate risks and capitalize on opportunities.
- **5. Monitor and Update:** Continuously track indicators that signal which scenario may be unfolding and adjust strategies accordingly.

Embracing Change as an Opportunity

Proactive leaders view change not as a threat but as an opportunity for innovation and growth. They foster an organizational mindset that welcomes change and encourages experimentation. This involves:

- **Promoting a Growth Mindset:** Encouraging continuous learning and viewing challenges as opportunities to develop new skills.
- **Investing in Innovation:** Allocating resources to research and development, and supporting initiatives that drive creative solutions.
- **Building Agile Structures**: Designing flexible organizational structures that can adapt quickly to new circumstances.

Case Study: Apple's Proactive Innovation

Background:

Apple Inc. exemplifies proactive leadership in anticipating market changes and driving innovation. Under the leadership of Steve Jobs and later Tim Cook, Apple has consistently anticipated consumer needs and technological trends.

Proactive Strategies:
- **Anticipating Market Shifts:** Recognized the potential of digital music, smartphones, and tablets before these markets matured, leading to the development of the iPod, iPhone, and iPad.
- **Investing in R&D:** Committed substantial resources to research and development, resulting in groundbreaking products and services.
- **Creating New Markets:** By anticipating consumer desires and leveraging emerging technologies, Apple didn't just adapt to change—it shaped it.

Outcome:

Apple's proactive approach has positioned it as a leader in innovation, consistently delivering products that redefine markets and consumer expectations.

Fostering a Culture of Proactive Problem-Solving

Central to proactive leadership is the cultivation of a culture where proactive problem-solving is not only encouraged but embedded in the organizational DNA. This involves creating an environment where team members feel empowered to identify and address challenges before they escalate.

Leaders can foster a culture of proactive problem-solving by:

- **Delegating Authority:** Granting team members the autonomy to make decisions within their areas of expertise.
- **Encouraging Ownership:** Instilling a sense of responsibility for outcomes, motivating employees to take initiative.
- **Providing Resources and Support:** Offering training, tools, and support systems that enable proactive action.

Equipping team members with the skills needed for proactive problem-solving is essential. This includes:

- **Critical Thinking Training:** Developing the ability to analyze situations, identify underlying issues, and anticipate potential challenges.
- **Innovation Workshops:** Facilitating sessions that encourage creative thinking and the exploration of new ideas.
- **Cross-Functional Collaboration:** Promoting collaboration across departments to bring diverse perspectives to problem-solving.

Recognition reinforces desired behaviors. Leaders should:

- **Celebrate Successes:** Publicly acknowledge individuals and teams who demonstrate proactive problem-solving.
- **Provide Incentives:** Offer rewards, promotions, or other incentives for proactive contributions.
- **Share Stories:** Highlight examples of proactive actions that led to positive outcomes, inspiring others to follow suit.

Effective communication is paramount in a culture of proactive problem-solving. Leaders must establish open channels for team members to:

- **Voice Concerns:** Encourage employees to speak up about potential issues or risks they observe.
- **Share Ideas:** Create forums for brainstorming and sharing innovative solutions.
- **Collaborate on Solutions:** Facilitate teamwork in developing and implementing proactive strategies.

By creating a safe and inclusive space for dialogue, leaders empower their teams to collectively navigate change and drive positive outcomes.

Case Study: Toyota's Continuous Improvement Culture

Background:

Toyota Motor Corporation is renowned for its culture of continuous improvement (Kaizen) and proactive problem-solving.

Proactive Strategies:

- **Empowering Employees:** All employees, from assembly line workers to executives, are encouraged to identify inefficiencies and suggest improvements.
- **Andon Cord System:** Workers can halt production to address quality issues immediately, preventing defects from progressing through the system.

- **Knowledge Sharing:** Regular meetings and communication channels facilitate the sharing of best practices and innovative ideas.

Outcome:

This proactive culture has contributed to Toyota's reputation for quality and efficiency, enabling the company to adapt and excel in a highly competitive industry.

Integrating the Holistic Intelligence Model

Shifting from reactive to proactive leadership aligns closely with several pillars of the Holistic Intelligence Model:

- **Practical Intelligence (PQ):** Applying knowledge effectively to anticipate challenges and implement proactive strategies.
- **Analytical Intelligence (AQ):** Utilizing critical thinking and data analysis to forecast trends and develop contingency plans.
- **Creative Intelligence (CrQ):** Encouraging innovative thinking to identify novel solutions and opportunities.
- **Cultural Intelligence (CQ):** Understanding diverse perspectives enhances the ability to anticipate changes in global markets and collaborate effectively.
- **Interpersonal Intelligence:** Building strong relationships and effective communication channels fosters a collaborative environment for proactive problem-solving.
- **Ethical Intelligence (EthQ):** Ensuring that proactive strategies align with ethical standards and organizational values builds trust and integrity.

Practical Strategies for Leaders

Developing Proactive Leadership Skills

1. Continuous Learning and Development
- **Stay Informed:** Keep abreast of industry developments, technological advancements, and global trends.
- **Professional Development:** Participate in leadership training, workshops, and seminars focused on strategic planning and foresight.

2. Enhancing Emotional Resilience
- **Mindfulness Practices:** Cultivate presence and awareness to respond thoughtfully rather than react impulsively.
- **Stress Management:** Develop coping strategies to maintain clarity under pressure.

3. Cultivating Strategic Thinking
- **Long-Term Visioning:** Set clear, long-term goals and align short-term actions accordingly.
- **Systems Thinking:** Understand the interdependencies within the organization and the broader ecosystem.

Implementing Organizational Practices

1. Establish Early Warning Systems
- **Key Performance Indicators (KPIs):** Define metrics that signal emerging issues or opportunities.
- **Feedback Loops:** Implement mechanisms for ongoing feedback from customers, employees, and stakeholders.

2. Encourage Experimentation
- **Pilot Programs:** Test new ideas on a small scale before wider implementation.
- **Fail Fast, Learn Faster:** Promote a culture where failures are seen as learning opportunities.

3. Strengthen Collaboration
- **Cross-Functional Teams:** Bring together diverse skill sets to tackle complex challenges.
- **Knowledge Management Systems:** Share information and insights across the organization to enhance collective intelligence.

Reflection Questions

1. Personal Leadership Style
- Do you tend to operate more reactively or proactively? Provide examples.
- What steps can you take to enhance your ability to anticipate change?

2. Organizational Culture
- How does your organization currently approach problem-solving?
- What changes can you implement to foster a more proactive culture?

3. Empowering Your Team
- In what ways can you empower your team members to take initiative?
- How can you recognize and reward proactive behaviors effectively?

Actionable Exercises

Exercise 1: Proactive Leadership Self-Assessment
- **Purpose:** Evaluate your current leadership approach and identify areas for development.
- **Steps:**
- **1. Reflect on Past Situations:** Identify instances where you reacted to problems versus anticipating them.
- **2. Assess Skills:** Rate yourself on skills such as foresight, strategic planning, and adaptability.
- **3. Set Goals:** Establish specific objectives to enhance your proactive leadership capabilities.

Exercise 2: Scenario Planning Workshop
- **Purpose:** Practice anticipating change and developing contingency plans.
- **Steps:**
- **1. Assemble a Team:** Include members from various departments.
- **2. Identify Key Drivers:** Determine factors that could significantly impact the organization.
- **3. Develop Scenarios:** Create detailed future scenarios based on these drivers.
- **4. Formulate Responses:** Develop strategies for each scenario.

Exercise 3: Proactive Problem-Solving Challenge
- **Purpose:** Encourage team members to identify and address potential issues proactively.
- **Steps:**
- **1. Set a Challenge:** Ask team members to identify areas for improvement within their workflows.

- **2. Provide Resources:** Offer support for implementing solutions.
- **3. Recognize Efforts:** Acknowledge contributions and share success stories.

Shifting from reactive to proactive leadership is essential for effectively navigating change in dynamic environments. By anticipating change, preparing for transitions, and fostering a culture of proactive problem-solving, leaders empower their organizations to not only survive but thrive in the face of evolving challenges.

Embracing proactive leadership requires a commitment to continuous learning, strategic foresight, and the empowerment of others. It involves integrating multiple intelligences—from analytical and practical to creative and interpersonal—to navigate complexity with agility and insight.

By adopting a proactive stance, leaders position their organizations at the forefront of innovation, ready to seize new opportunities and shape the future. This approach fosters resilience, drives growth, and cultivates a culture of excellence that sustains success in an ever-changing world.

Empowering and Supporting Your Team

- "Empowerment is the foundation of a resilient team; when leaders nurture their team's strengths, they cultivate a collective capacity to thrive amidst change."

In times of change, the role of a leader extends far beyond making strategic decisions; it encompasses empowering and supporting the entire team to navigate the uncertainties ahead. Effective leadership during transitions hinges on the ability to foster a supportive environment where team members feel valued, heard, and equipped to adapt. This section delves into the critical aspects of providing clear communication and guidance, recognizing and addressing team members' concerns, and cultivating a resilient team culture.

Providing Clear Communication and Guidance

Clear and transparent communication is the cornerstone of effective leadership, especially during periods of change. When team members are well-informed about the vision, goals, and strategies guiding the organization's response to change, it instills confidence and trust in leadership. Transparent communication mitigates uncertainties and aligns everyone toward common objectives.

Key Strategies for Effective Communication:

1. Articulate a Compelling Vision:
- **Define Clear Objectives:** Clearly outline what the organization aims to achieve during and after the change.
- **Align with Values:** Ensure that the vision resonates with the team's values and the organization's mission.
- **Inspire and Motivate:** Use language that energizes and mobilizes the team toward collective goals.

2. Utilize Multiple Communication Channels:
- **Regular Team Meetings:** Schedule consistent meetings to provide updates and address questions.
- **Digital Platforms:** Leverage emails, intranet, and collaboration tools to disseminate information promptly.
- **Visual Aids:** Use presentations, infographics, and dashboards to make complex information accessible.

3. Encourage Open Dialogue:
- **Two-Way Communication:** Foster an environment where team members feel comfortable sharing their thoughts and feedback.
- **Active Listening:** Demonstrate genuine interest in employees' perspectives by listening attentively and responding thoughtfully.
- **Accessibility:** Make yourself available for one-on-one conversations, signaling your commitment to individual concerns.

4. Set Clear Expectations and Provide Guidance:
- **Define Roles and Responsibilities:** Clarify what is expected from each team member during the transition.

- **Provide Resources:** Offer the necessary tools, training, and support to fulfill new or adjusted roles.
- **Continuous Feedback:** Give regular, constructive feedback to guide performance and acknowledge progress.

Case Study: Microsoft's Cultural Transformation

Background:

When Satya Nadella became CEO of Microsoft in 2014, he recognized the need for a cultural shift to foster innovation and collaboration.

Leadership Actions:

- **Transparent Communication:** Nadella openly communicated the new vision, focusing on a "growth mindset" and breaking down silos within the company.
- **Empowering Employees:** He encouraged employees to embrace learning and take initiative, providing guidance and support for new ideas.
- **Regular Engagement:** Nadella prioritized connecting with employees at all levels through meetings, emails, and company-wide events.

Outcome:

Under his leadership, Microsoft experienced a resurgence in innovation and employee engagement, driving significant growth and revitalizing the company's culture.

Recognizing and Addressing Team Members' Concerns

During periods of change, team members may experience a range of emotions, including anxiety, uncertainty, and resistance. Effective leaders are attuned to these sentiments and take proactive steps to address them. Recognizing and validating these feelings is essential in maintaining morale and fostering a supportive environment.

Strategies for Addressing Concerns:

1. Create a Safe Space for Expression:

- **Psychological Safety:** Ensure that team members feel safe to voice their thoughts without fear of negative repercussions.
- **Confidential Conversations:** Offer private meetings for individuals uncomfortable sharing in group settings.
- **Anonymity Options:** Provide channels for anonymous feedback if necessary.

2. Practice Active Listening:

- **Empathetic Engagement:** Listen with the intent to understand, not just to respond.
- **Acknowledge Emotions:** Validate feelings by expressing understanding and empathy.
- **Avoid Interruptions:** Allow team members to fully express their concerns before offering input.

3. Provide Emotional Support:

- **Offer Reassurance:** Address fears related to job security, workload, or capability to adapt.

- **Connect to Resources:** Refer employees to support services such as counseling or employee assistance programs.
- **Demonstrate Understanding:** Share personal experiences with change to build rapport.

4. Take Proactive Measures:

- **Identify Potential Issues:** Anticipate areas where concerns may arise and address them early.
- **Adjust Workloads:** Be mindful of added pressures and redistribute tasks if necessary.
- **Facilitate Training:** Provide opportunities for skill development to ease transitions.

Case Study: Southwest Airlines' Employee-Centric Approach

Background:

Southwest Airlines has long been recognized for its strong organizational culture and commitment to employee well-being.

Leadership Actions:

- **Open Communication:** Leadership maintains transparency about company performance and changes affecting employees.
- **Employee Empowerment:** Staff at all levels are encouraged to make decisions that enhance customer experiences.
- **Support Systems:** The company offers robust support programs, including professional development and wellness initiatives.

Outcome:

Southwest's focus on empowering and supporting employees has resulted in high employee satisfaction, low turnover rates, and strong organizational performance, even during industry downturns.

Cultivating a Resilient Team Culture

Building Trust and Mutual Respect

Empowering and supporting the team during change fosters a culture of trust and mutual respect. Leaders can cultivate this environment by:

- **Consistency:** Aligning actions with words to build credibility.
- **Inclusivity:** Valuing diverse perspectives and involving team members in decision-making processes.
- **Recognition:** Celebrating achievements and acknowledging individual and team contributions.

Encouraging Collaboration and Teamwork

Promote a collaborative culture where team members support one another:

- **Team-Building Activities:** Organize events that strengthen relationships and foster camaraderie.
- **Cross-Training Opportunities:** Encourage knowledge sharing and skill development across roles.
- **Collective Problem-Solving:** Involve the team in identifying challenges and brainstorming solutions.

Integrating the Holistic Intelligence Model

Empowering and supporting your team aligns with several pillars of the Holistic Intelligence Model:

1. Interpersonal Intelligence:
- **Effective Communication:** Strengthen relationships through clear communication and active listening.
- **Empathy and Understanding:** Build connections by recognizing and addressing emotional needs.

2. Intrapersonal Intelligence:
- **Self-Awareness:** Leaders must understand their own emotions and biases to support others effectively.
- **Emotional Regulation:** Managing personal stress enables leaders to remain composed and supportive.

3. Emotional Resilience (ER):
- **Modeling Resilience:** Demonstrate adaptability and a positive attitude toward change.
- **Supporting Team Resilience:** Provide resources and encouragement to help team members cope with challenges.

4. Ethical Intelligence (EthQ):
- **Integrity:** Uphold ethical standards in all interactions.
- **Fairness:** Ensure equitable treatment and opportunities for all team members.

Practical Strategies and Exercises

Exercise 1: Communication Audit

- **Purpose:** Evaluate the effectiveness of current communication practices.
- **Steps:**
- 1. **Gather Feedback:** Survey team members on their perceptions of communication clarity and transparency.
- 2. **Identify Gaps**: Analyze the feedback to pinpoint areas needing improvement.
- 3. **Develop an Action Plan:** Implement strategies to enhance communication based on insights gained.

Exercise 2: Empathy Mapping

- **Purpose:** Understand team members' perspectives and emotions during change.
- **Steps:**
- 1. **Create Empathy Maps:** For different team roles, map out what individuals might be thinking, feeling, saying, and doing.
- 2. **Identify Common Concerns:** Look for patterns or shared anxieties.
- 3. **Address Needs:** Develop targeted support measures to alleviate concerns.

Exercise 3: Team Feedback Sessions

- **Purpose:** Foster open dialogue and collective problem-solving.
- **Steps:**
- 1. **Schedule Regular Meetings:** Create a consistent forum for team discussions.

- **2. Set Ground Rules:** Establish guidelines to ensure respectful and constructive conversations.
- **3. Facilitate Discussions:** Encourage participation and guide the conversation to focus on solutions.

Reflection Questions

1. Communication Effectiveness:

- How clear and transparent is your current communication with your team?
- What barriers might be hindering effective communication, and how can you address them?

2. Understanding Team Concerns:

- What strategies are you using to recognize and address your team members' concerns?
- How can you improve your active listening skills to better support your team?

3. Empowerment Practices:

- In what ways are you empowering your team to take ownership during change?
- How do you recognize and celebrate your team members' contributions?

—

Empowering and supporting your team is an integral aspect of leadership, particularly during times of change. By providing clear communication and guidance, leaders create a transparent environment where team members understand the direction and their roles within it. Recognizing and addressing team members' concerns fosters trust, mitigates anxieties, and strengthens the leader-team relationship.

Leaders who prioritize the well-being and development of their team cultivate a resilient and adaptable workforce. This not only facilitates smoother transitions during change but also enhances overall organizational performance. By integrating principles from the Holistic Intelligence Model, leaders can develop the interpersonal and intrapersonal skills necessary to navigate the human dynamics of change effectively.

Additional Insights

Research Findings
- **Impact of Communication on Change Success:**
- Studies have shown that effective communication is a critical factor in the success of change initiatives. Organizations with strong communication practices are more likely to meet their change objectives (Project Management Institute).
- **Employee Engagement and Performance:**
- Engaged employees are more productive, provide better customer service, and are more likely to remain with the organization (Gallup).

Quotes to Inspire

Simon Sinek: "Leadership is not about being in charge. It is about taking care of those in your charge."

Maya Angelou: "People will forget what you said, people will forget what you did, but people will never forget how you made them feel."

John C. Maxwell: "People buy into the leader before they buy into the vision."

Leveraging Technology and Innovation

- "Innovation is the bridge between today's challenges and tomorrow's opportunities; by harnessing technology, leaders can transform uncertainty into a landscape of growth."

In an era defined by rapid technological advancement and constant disruption, leaders must harness the power of innovation and technology to navigate change effectively. The integration of technology and a culture of innovation are not just competitive advantages—they are necessities for survival and growth in today's dynamic business landscape. This section explores strategies for embracing technological solutions to enhance agility and outlines how to foster a culture of innovation and experimentation within the organization.

Embracing Technological Solutions for Increased Agility

Technology serves as a catalyst for organizational agility, enabling businesses to respond swiftly and effectively to change. Embracing technological solutions allows organizations to:

- **Enhance Operational Efficiency:** Automate routine tasks, reduce errors, and streamline processes.

- **Facilitate Collaboration:** Connect teams across geographies and time zones, fostering seamless communication.
- **Enable Data-Driven Decision-Making:** Access real-time insights to inform strategies and actions.
- **Scale Resources Flexibly:** Adjust operations quickly in response to market demands.

Key Technological Solutions

1. Cloud Computing and Infrastructure

Scalability and Flexibility: Cloud-based platforms offer on-demand resources, allowing organizations to scale up or down as needed.

Cost Efficiency: Reduce capital expenditures by leveraging cloud services instead of investing in physical infrastructure.

Accessibility: Enable remote access to systems and data, supporting distributed workforces.

2. Enterprise Resource Planning (ERP) Systems

Integrated Processes: Unify core business processes across departments, improving coordination and efficiency.

Real-Time Insights: Provide dashboards and analytics for informed decision-making.

Customization: Tailor solutions to specific industry needs and organizational structures.

3. Project Management and Collaboration Tools

Centralized Communication: Tools like Slack, Microsoft Teams, and Asana facilitate team collaboration and information sharing.

Task Management: Track progress, assign responsibilities, and manage deadlines effectively.

Remote Work Support: Enable virtual teams to collaborate seamlessly.

4. Artificial Intelligence (AI) and Machine Learning (ML)

Automation: Automate complex tasks, from customer service chatbots to predictive maintenance.

Data Analytics: Analyze large datasets to uncover patterns, trends, and insights.

Personalization: Enhance customer experiences through tailored recommendations and services.

5. Internet of Things (IoT)

Operational Efficiency: Use connected devices to monitor and optimize processes in real-time.

Data Collection: Gather valuable data from physical assets for analysis and improvement.

Enhanced Connectivity: Integrate physical and digital systems for comprehensive oversight.

Strategies for Effective Technological Integration

1. Stay Informed About Emerging Technologies

- **Continuous Learning:** Leaders should invest time in understanding technological trends and their potential impact.
- **Industry Networks:** Participate in industry forums, conferences, and professional networks to stay updated.
- **Technology Audits:** Regularly assess current technology stacks to identify gaps and opportunities.

2. Align Technology with Business Goals

- **Strategic Planning:** Ensure that technology investments support the organization's strategic objectives.
- **Cross-Functional Collaboration:** Involve stakeholders from different departments to understand needs and integrate solutions effectively.
- **Return on Investment (ROI) Analysis:** Evaluate the potential benefits against costs to prioritize initiatives.

3. Invest in Talent and Skills Development

- **Upskilling Employees:** Provide training programs to develop technical competencies among staff.
- **Attracting Talent:** Hire individuals with expertise in key technological areas.
- **Leadership Development:** Equip leaders with the knowledge to make informed technology decisions.

4. Implement Change Management Practices

- **Stakeholder Engagement:** Communicate the purpose and benefits of new technologies to gain buy-in.

- **Pilot Programs:** Test technologies on a small scale before full implementation to identify challenges.
- **Feedback Mechanisms:** Establish channels for users to provide input and report issues.

Case Study: General Electric's Digital Transformation

Background:

General Electric (GE), a multinational conglomerate, recognized the need to embrace digital technology to stay competitive in industries like aviation, energy, and healthcare.

Actions Taken:

- **Investment in Predix Platform:** GE developed Predix, an industrial IoT platform, to collect and analyze data from machinery.
- **Data-Driven Services:** Offered predictive maintenance and performance optimization services to customers.
- **Cultural Shift:** Promoted a digital mindset across the organization through training and leadership initiatives.

Outcomes:

- **Enhanced Customer Value:** Provided innovative solutions that improved customer operations.
- **Operational Efficiency:** Optimized internal processes through data insights.
- **Market Positioning:** Positioned GE as a leader in industrial digital transformation.

Encouraging a Culture of Innovation and Experimentation

Fostering a culture of innovation is paramount to an organization's ability to thrive amidst change. An innovative culture enables organizations to:

- **Adapt Quickly:** Respond to market shifts with creative solutions.
- **Drive Growth:** Develop new products, services, and business models.
- **Engage Employees:** Inspire and motivate teams through meaningful work.

Strategies to Foster Innovation

1. Leadership Commitment and Role Modeling

- **Lead by Example:** Leaders should demonstrate a willingness to explore new ideas and take calculated risks.
- **Communicate Vision:** Articulate the importance of innovation in achieving organizational goals.
- **Allocate Time and Resources:** Dedicate budget and time for innovation initiatives.

2. Empower Employees

- **Autonomy:** Grant employees the freedom to experiment and make decisions.
- **Skill Development:** Provide training in creative thinking, problem-solving, and design thinking methodologies.
- **Access to Tools:** Supply the necessary technology and resources to pursue innovative projects.

3. Establish Innovation Processes and Platforms

- **Idea Management Systems:** Implement platforms where employees can submit and collaborate on ideas.
- **Innovation Labs and Incubators:** Create dedicated spaces for developing and testing new concepts.
- **Cross-Functional Teams:** Encourage collaboration across departments to blend diverse perspectives.

4. Encourage Risk-Taking and Learn from Failures

- **Accept Failures as Learning Opportunities:** Shift the mindset from penalizing failures to analyzing them for insights.
- **Celebrate Efforts:** Recognize attempts at innovation, regardless of the outcome.
- **Iterative Development:** Promote rapid prototyping and iterative improvements.

5. Recognition and Rewards

- **Incentive Programs:** Offer rewards for innovative ideas that contribute to organizational goals.
- **Public Acknowledgment:** Highlight contributions in company communications and events.
- **Career Advancement:** Provide opportunities for growth and leadership roles in innovation initiatives.

Case Study: 3M's Culture of Innovation

Background:

3M, a multinational conglomerate, is renowned for its innovative products across various industries.

Innovation Strategies:

- **15% Rule:** Employees are allowed to spend 15% of their work time on projects of their choosing.
- **Cross-Pollination of Ideas:** Encouraged collaboration between different business units.
- **Recognition Programs:** Established awards and incentives for innovative contributions.

Outcomes:

- **Product Development:** Innovations like Post-it Notes and Scotch Tape emerged from employee initiatives.
- **Sustained Growth:** Continual development of new products kept 3M competitive and relevant.
- **Employee Engagement:** High levels of job satisfaction and retention due to the empowering culture.

Integrating the Holistic Intelligence Model

Leveraging technology and fostering innovation align with multiple pillars of the Holistic Intelligence Model:

Creative Intelligence (CrQ):

- **Encouraging Creativity:** Cultivating an environment where new ideas are generated and explored.
- **Problem-Solving:** Applying creative thinking to overcome challenges and develop innovative solutions.

Analytical Intelligence (AQ):

- **Data-Driven Decisions:** Utilizing analytical skills to interpret data and inform technology adoption.
- **Strategic Analysis:** Evaluating technological trends and their potential impact on the organization.

Practical Intelligence (PQ):
- **Application of Technology:** Effectively implementing technological solutions to enhance operations.
- **Operational Efficiency:** Streamlining processes through practical use of innovations.

Emotional Resilience (ER):
- **Managing Change:** Supporting teams in adapting to new technologies and ways of working.
- **Overcoming Resistance:** Addressing fears and uncertainties associated with technological changes.

Cultural Intelligence (CQ):
- **Global Collaboration:** Leveraging technology to connect diverse teams across cultures.
- **Inclusive Innovation:** Ensuring that innovation efforts consider and respect cultural differences.

Ethical Intelligence (EthQ):
- **Responsible Innovation:** Considering ethical implications of technology use, such as data privacy and AI bias.
- **Sustainable Practices:** Embracing technologies that promote environmental and social responsibility.

Practical Strategies and Exercises

Exercise 1: Technology Assessment and Roadmap Development
- **Purpose:** Identify technological needs and create a strategic plan for implementation.
- **Steps:**
- 1. **Assess Current Technology Stack:**

- Inventory existing technologies and evaluate their effectiveness.
- Identify gaps and areas for improvement.
- **2. Define Business Objectives:**
- Align technology initiatives with strategic goals.
- Prioritize areas where technology can have the most significant impact.
- **3. Research Emerging Technologies:**
- Explore technologies relevant to your industry.
- Evaluate potential benefits and challenges.
- **4. Develop a Technology Roadmap:**
- Outline short-term and long-term technology adoption plans.
- Assign timelines, responsibilities, and resources.
- **5. Monitor and Review:**
- Regularly update the roadmap based on progress and changing needs.
- Adjust strategies as necessary.

Exercise 2: Innovation Workshop

- **Purpose:** Foster creative thinking and generate innovative ideas.
- **Steps:**
- **1. Set Objectives:**
- Define the focus area or problem to address during the workshop.
- **2. Assemble Diverse Teams:**
- Include participants from various departments and backgrounds.
- **3. Facilitate Brainstorming Sessions:**

- Use techniques like mind mapping, brainstorming, and the SCAMPER method (Substitute, Combine, Adapt, Modify, Put to another use, Eliminate, Reverse).
- **4. Develop Prototypes or Concepts:**
- Encourage teams to create mock-ups or outlines of their ideas.
- **5. Present and Evaluate Ideas:**
- Have teams share their concepts.
- Provide constructive feedback and select ideas for further development.

Exercise 3: Establishing an Innovation Recognition Program

- **Purpose:** Encourage and reward innovative contributions.
- **Steps:**
- **1. Define Criteria:**
- Establish clear guidelines for what constitutes innovation in your organization.
- **2. Create Nomination and Selection Processes:**
- Allow for peer and management nominations.
- Form a committee to review and select recipients.
- **3. Determine Rewards:**
- Decide on appropriate incentives, such as bonuses, promotions, or public recognition.
- **4. Communicate the Program:**
- Announce the program details to all employees.
- Encourage participation and highlight the importance of innovation.
- **5. Celebrate Achievements:**
- Host events or ceremonies to honor recipients.
- Share success stories to inspire others.

Reflection Questions

1. Technology Integration:
- How effectively is your organization currently leveraging technology to enhance agility?
- What barriers exist to adopting new technologies, and how can they be overcome?

2. Innovation Culture:
- In what ways does your organization's culture support or hinder innovation?
- How can you, as a leader, foster an environment that encourages experimentation and creativity?

3. Personal Leadership:
- Are you staying informed about technological advancements relevant to your industry?
- How do you model innovative thinking and openness to new ideas for your team?

—

Leveraging technology and innovation is essential for organizations seeking to navigate change successfully. By embracing technological solutions, leaders enhance operational agility, enabling their organizations to respond swiftly to evolving demands. Cultivating a culture of innovation empowers teams to think creatively, embrace risks, and drive sustainable growth.

Leaders play a pivotal role in integrating technology and fostering innovation. By aligning technological initiatives with strategic goals, investing in talent development, and promoting an innovative culture, leaders position their organizations at the forefront of their industries.

Integrating principles from the Holistic Intelligence Model ensures that technological and innovative efforts are balanced with ethical considerations, cultural awareness, and practical application. This holistic approach enables organizations to harness the full potential of technology and innovation, driving success in dynamic environments.

Additional Insights

Emerging Technologies to Watch

Blockchain Technology:

- **Applications:** Beyond cryptocurrencies, blockchain can enhance supply chain transparency, security, and efficiency.
- **Implications:** Offers opportunities for new business models and trust mechanisms.

Augmented Reality (AR) and Virtual Reality (VR):

- **Applications:** Training, customer experiences, and product design.
- **Implications:** Enhances engagement and can reduce costs through virtual simulations.

5G Connectivity:

- **Applications:** Enables faster data transfer, supporting IoT devices and real-time analytics.
- **Implications:** Facilitates more sophisticated technologies and services.

Ethical Considerations in Technology

Data Privacy and Security:
- Ensure compliance with regulations like GDPR.
- Protect customer and employee data through robust cybersecurity measures.

AI Ethics:
- Address biases in algorithms.
- Ensure transparency and accountability in AI decision-making processes.

Environmental Impact:
- Consider the sustainability of technology solutions.
- Promote green IT practices to reduce the carbon footprint.

Quotes to Inspire

Albert Einstein: "We cannot solve our problems with the same thinking we used when we created them."

Peter Drucker: "The greatest danger in times of turbulence is not the turbulence—it is to act with yesterday's logic."

Steve Jobs: "Innovation distinguishes between a leader and a follower."

Case Study 1: The Adaptable Leader in Action

- "Through decisive action and unwavering flexibility, the adaptable leader turns every challenge into an opportunity for transformation and growth."

In this case study, we delve into the exemplary leadership journey of Johnathan Hayes, a seasoned executive known for his remarkable adaptability and resilience in the face of change. Understanding the background, experience, and leadership style of Johnathan provides valuable insights into the practical application of adaptive leadership in dynamic business environments.

Background, Experience, and Leadership Style

Johnathan Hayes brings a wealth of experience to the table, having navigated diverse industries and held leadership positions in both startups and established corporations. His early career in technology startups exposed him to the fast-paced, ever-changing landscape of the tech industry. This formative experience instilled in him a deep appreciation for adaptability and a proactive approach to change.

Over the years, Johnathan's journey led him to leadership roles in Fortune 500 companies, where he confronted the complexities of managing large teams and diverse stakeholders. His ability to guide organizations through mergers, acquisitions, and industry disruptions showcases his adeptness at leading in turbulent times.

One of Johnathan's distinctive leadership traits is his inclusive and collaborative style. He fosters an environment where diverse perspectives are valued, encouraging cross-functional teams to collaborate on innovative solutions. This approach not only enhances problem-solving capabilities but also builds a culture of adaptability and continuous learning.

Furthermore, Johnathan embodies a growth mindset, viewing challenges as opportunities for development. He instills this outlook in his teams, emphasizing the importance of embracing change as a catalyst for growth. Through mentorship and coaching, he empowers his team members to develop their own adaptive leadership skills, ensuring the organization as a whole is poised to thrive in dynamic environments.

Johnathan's leadership journey serves as a compelling case study, illustrating the practical application of adaptive leadership principles. By examining his background, experiences, and leadership style, leaders can glean actionable insights for honing their own adaptability and resilience in the face of change. This section sets the stage for a deep dive into the key situations that showcase Johnathan's exceptional adaptability and the strategies that can be extracted for application in diverse business contexts.

Key Situations Showcasing Adaptability

Let's dissect pivotal moments in Johnathan Hayes' leadership journey that vividly exemplify his extraordinary adaptability. These situations illuminate his ability to make effective decisions in dynamic environments and showcase his unwavering resilience in the face of rapid change.

Embracing Technological Disruption

Early in Johnathan's career, he found himself at the helm of a technology startup faced with a disruptive innovation that threatened to render their existing product obsolete. Instead of resisting change, Johnathan astutely recognized the potential for innovation and swiftly pivoted the company's focus. By marshaling the team's collective creativity and expertise, he successfully transitioned the organization towards a new, cutting-edge solution that not only addressed the evolving market needs but also propelled the company to the forefront of the industry.

Navigating Market Volatility

During a period of economic downturn, Johnathan was leading a division within a multinational corporation. The rapidly changing market conditions necessitated a shift in strategy to safeguard the division's viability. Rather than succumbing to uncertainty, Johnathan methodically assessed the available data, consulted with cross-functional teams, and made the strategic decision to diversify the division's product offerings. This timely intervention not only stabilized the division's revenue streams but also positioned it for sustained growth once the market rebounded.

Leading Through Mergers and Acquisitions

In a significant turning point for his career, Johnathan found himself at the forefront of a high-stakes merger between two industry giants. The merger brought with it a myriad of challenges, from aligning organizational cultures to integrating disparate systems and processes. Recognizing the need for a harmonized approach, Johnathan orchestrated a meticulous transition plan, emphasizing open communication, cultural sensitivity, and a clear strategic vision. His adept management of this complex process not only ensured a seamless integration but also solidified his reputation as a leader capable of steering organizations through transformative change.

Responding to Global Crises

The emergence of a global crisis posed unprecedented challenges for Johnathan and his team. The sudden and unpredictable nature of the crisis demanded rapid decision-making and a high degree of adaptability. Johnathan responded by swiftly mobilizing his team, leveraging their collective expertise to devise innovative solutions, and demonstrating a steadfast commitment to the well-being of his employees. His poised leadership during this turbulent period not only safeguarded the organization's operations but also galvanized the team's sense of purpose and unity.

These key situations in Johnathan's leadership journey serve as illuminating case studies, offering valuable insights into the practical application of adaptability in complex, real-world scenarios. By dissecting these moments of effective decision-making and unwavering resilience, leaders can extract actionable strategies for navigating their own dynamic business environments.

Extracting Insights and Strategies

Let's distill the invaluable lessons learned from Johnathan Hayes' experiences as an adaptable leader. By examining his journey, we uncover a wealth of practical takeaways that can be applied by leaders navigating their own dynamic environments.

Embrace Change as an Opportunity for Growth

One of the most resounding lessons from Johnathan's journey is the transformative power of viewing change not as a threat, but as an opportunity for growth. In each of the key situations we explored, Johnathan exhibited a remarkable ability to not only adapt to change but to actively seek out the potential for innovation and improvement. This mindset shift propelled his organizations to new heights, illustrating the profound impact a growth-oriented perspective can have on navigating dynamic environments.

Prioritize Clear Communication and Transparency

Throughout Johnathan's leadership tenure, a consistent thread emerges: the prioritization of clear communication and transparency. Whether leading through mergers, responding to crises, or navigating technological disruption, Johnathan understood the critical importance of keeping stakeholders informed and engaged. His commitment to open dialogue fostered trust, mitigated uncertainty, and ultimately paved the way for successful outcomes.

Cultivate a Culture of Collaboration and Adaptability

Johnathan's leadership style underscores the significance of cultivating a culture characterized by collaboration and adaptability. By empowering his teams to contribute their diverse perspectives and expertise, he harnessed the collective intelligence of the organization to tackle complex challenges. This collaborative approach not only enhanced problem-solving capabilities but also instilled a sense of ownership and resilience within the teams.

Practical Takeaways for Leaders Navigating Change

One of the key strategies that emerges from Johnathan's experiences is the importance of proactive scenario planning. By envisioning potential future scenarios and developing corresponding strategies, leaders can position themselves to respond swiftly and effectively to change. This forward-thinking approach enables organizations to navigate uncertainty with confidence and agility.

Johnathan's journey emphasizes the value of fostering a learning-oriented culture within an organization. By creating an environment where curiosity is encouraged, and continuous learning is prioritized, leaders can equip their teams with the skills and mindset necessary to adapt to evolving circumstances. This culture of learning becomes a powerful asset in times of change, enabling organizations to stay ahead of the curve.

Perhaps one of the most profound takeaways from Johnathan's experiences is the importance of leading with empathy and resilience. By demonstrating genuine concern for the well-being of team members and steadfastly navigating challenges, leaders can inspire confidence, unity, and a shared sense of purpose. This empathetic leadership style not only bolsters team morale but also fortifies the organization's collective resolve in the face of change.

In conclusion, Johnathan Hayes' journey as an adaptable leader offers a treasure trove of insights and strategies for leaders navigating change. By embracing change as an opportunity for growth, prioritizing clear communication, cultivating a culture of collaboration, and adopting a proactive mindset, leaders can chart a course of resilience in dynamic environments. These practical takeaways serve as a blueprint for leaders seeking to not only survive but thrive amidst the whirlwind of change.

Guided Self-Assessment: Evaluating Your Adaptability

- "Self-awareness is the compass that guides us through change; by understanding our strengths and areas for growth, we chart a path toward greater adaptability."

In a world of constant change, understanding and enhancing your adaptability is crucial for personal and professional growth. This section invites you on a journey of self-discovery, providing a comprehensive self-assessment designed to evaluate and strengthen your capacity to navigate dynamic environments. By reflecting on past experiences and identifying areas for improvement, you'll gain valuable insights into your adaptability, empowering you to thrive amidst flux.

Reflecting on Past Experiences with Change

Reflection is a powerful tool for personal development. By examining your past experiences with change, you can uncover patterns in your responses, recognize strengths to build upon, and identify areas that may benefit from development. This introspective process serves as a foundation for enhancing your adaptability.

Guided Reflection Exercise

1. Choose Significant Experiences

Select 2-3 significant moments in your personal or professional life where you encountered substantial change. These could include:

- **Career Transitions:** Starting a new job, changing careers, or experiencing organizational restructuring.
- **Personal Life Changes:** Moving to a new city, significant relationship changes, or health challenges.
- **Unexpected Events:** Navigating crises, market disruptions, or technological advancements impacting your role.

2. Analyze Your Responses

For each experience, consider the following questions:

Emotional Reactions:

- How did you feel when the change was introduced?
- Did you experience excitement, anxiety, resistance, or curiosity?

Behavioral Responses:

- What actions did you take to adapt to the change?
- Did you seek information, resist the change, or proactively engage with new opportunities?

Cognitive Processing:

- How did you perceive the change?
- Did you view it as a threat or an opportunity?

Outcome Reflections:
- What was the result of your response to the change?
- What did you learn from the experience?

3. Identify Patterns and Themes

After analyzing each experience, look for commonalities:

- **Emotional Patterns:** Do you consistently feel a certain way when faced with change?
- **Behavioral Tendencies:** Are there habitual actions you take?
- **Mindset Indicators:** Do you have a fixed or growth mindset regarding change?

Case Example

Scenario: Transition to Remote Work
- **Emotional Reaction:** Initial anxiety due to unfamiliar technology and loss of routine.
- **Behavioral Response:** Delayed setting up a home office, leading to decreased productivity.
- **Cognitive Processing:** Viewed remote work as a temporary inconvenience.
- **Outcome Reflection:** Recognized the need to adapt and eventually established an effective work-from-home routine.

Pattern Identified: Initial resistance to technological changes but eventual adaptation when recognizing long-term benefits.

Identifying Areas for Growth and Improvement

Assessing Your Adaptability Skills

Based on your reflections, consider the following dimensions of adaptability:

1. **Emotional Resilience (ER):** Ability to manage emotions and remain composed during change.
2. **Cognitive Flexibility:** Capacity to adjust your thinking and embrace new ideas.
3. **Learning Orientation:** Openness to acquiring new skills and knowledge.
4. **Proactive Problem-Solving:** Tendency to anticipate challenges and develop solutions.
5. **Risk Tolerance:** Comfort with uncertainty and taking calculated risks.
6. **Interpersonal Skills:** Effectiveness in communicating and collaborating with others during transitions.
7. **Cultural Intelligence (CQ):** Ability to navigate and respect diverse perspectives in changing environments.

Self-Evaluation Exercise

Rate yourself on a scale of 1 to 5 for each adaptability dimension:

- **1:** Significant development needed
- **2:** Some development needed
- **3:** Adequate
- **4:** Strong

- **5:** Exceptional

Example:
- Emotional Resilience: 3
- Cognitive Flexibility: 2
- Learning Orientation: 4
- Proactive Problem-Solving: 3
- Risk Tolerance: 2
- Interpersonal Skills: 4
- Cultural Intelligence: 3

Identifying Strengths and Development Areas

- **Strengths:** Areas where you scored 4 or 5 are your strengths. Leverage these in adapting to change.
- **Development Areas:** Scores of 1 to 3 indicate opportunities for growth.

Setting Personal Development Goals

For each development area:

- 1. **Define Specific Goals:**
- **Example:** Improve cognitive flexibility by embracing new ideas and perspectives.
- 2. **Outline Action Steps:**
- **Seek Diverse Experiences:** Engage with people from different backgrounds.
- **Practice Open-Mindedness:** Challenge your assumptions regularly.
- **Learn New Skills:** Enroll in courses that push you out of your comfort zone.
- 3. **Establish a Timeline:**

- Set achievable milestones over the next 3 to 6 months.
- **4. Monitor Progress:**
- Reflect on your growth periodically and adjust your plan as needed.

Overcoming Barriers to Adaptability

Recognizing Potential Obstacles

Identify barriers that may impede your adaptability:

- **Fixed Mindset:** Believing that abilities are static.
- **Fear of Failure:** Avoiding risks due to potential negative outcomes.
- **Comfort Zone Dependence:** Preferring familiarity over new experiences.
- **Limiting Beliefs:** Holding assumptions that restrict growth (e.g., "I'm not tech-savvy").

Strategies to Overcome Obstacles

- 1. **Adopt a Growth Mindset:**
- Embrace the belief that abilities can be developed through effort and learning.
- Replace limiting beliefs with empowering ones.
- 2. **Build Emotional Resilience:**
- Practice stress management techniques like mindfulness or deep-breathing exercises.
- Seek support from mentors or peers.
- 3. **Increase Risk Tolerance:**
- Start with small risks to build confidence.
- Reflect on past successes to reinforce your ability to handle uncertainty.

- 4. **Expand Your Comfort Zone:**
- Set challenges that gradually push your boundaries.
- Celebrate small victories to encourage continued growth.
- 5. **Seek Feedback and Support:**
- Request constructive feedback from trusted colleagues or friends.
- Join support groups or professional networks focused on personal development.

Integrating the Holistic Intelligence Model

The 8 Pillars of the Holistic Intelligence Model provide a framework to enhance your adaptability:

- **Emotional Resilience (ER):** Strengthen your ability to cope with stress and recover from setbacks.
- **Creative Intelligence (CrQ):** Foster innovative thinking to generate new solutions.
- **Practical Intelligence (PQ):** Apply knowledge effectively in real-world situations.
- **Cultural Intelligence (CQ):** Improve your effectiveness in diverse cultural settings.
- **Intrapersonal Intelligence:** Deepen self-awareness and self-regulation.
- **Interpersonal Intelligence:** Enhance communication and relationship-building skills.
- **Ethical Intelligence (EthQ):** Uphold integrity and ethical principles during change.
- **Analytical Intelligence (AQ):** Develop critical thinking and problem-solving abilities.

Action Plan Example

Goal: Enhance Intrapersonal Intelligence to improve self-awareness during change.

Action Steps:
- **Journaling:** Reflect daily on thoughts and emotions related to change.
- **Mindfulness Practice:** Engage in meditation to increase present-moment awareness.
- **Assessments:** Utilize tools like William Stanek's Resilient Growth Self-Assessment and the 8 Pillars of Leadership: Self-Assessment to gain insights.

Practical Exercises and Tools

Exercise 1: Adaptability Journal

Purpose: Track your experiences and growth over time.

Instructions:
- **Daily Entries:** Note situations where you faced change and how you responded.
- **Reflections:** Analyze what went well and what could be improved.
- **Progress Tracking:** Review entries weekly to identify trends and adjust your action plan.

Exercise 2: Strengths and Weaknesses Analysis

Purpose: Gain a balanced understanding of your capabilities.

Instructions:

- **List Strengths:** Identify at least five strengths related to adaptability.
- **List Weaknesses:** Identify at least five areas for improvement.
- **Action Planning:** For each weakness, outline steps to develop it into a strength.

Exercise 3: Visualization Technique

Purpose: Mentally rehearse adapting successfully to change.

Instructions:

- **Relaxation:** Find a quiet space and relax your mind.
- Imagery: Visualize a future scenario involving significant change.
- **Positive Outcome:** Imagine yourself navigating the change confidently and effectively.
- **Reflection:** After visualization, note any insights or feelings that arise.

Reflection Questions

1. Self-Perception:

- How do you currently perceive your ability to adapt to change?
- What past successes can you draw upon to boost your confidence?

2. Emotional Responses:

- What emotions frequently arise when you face change?
- How can you manage these emotions more effectively?

3. Mindset and Attitudes:
- Do you approach change with a fixed or growth mindset?
- How can you cultivate a more growth-oriented perspective?

4. Support Systems:
- Who can support you in your journey toward greater adaptability?
- How can you leverage relationships to facilitate your growth?

5. Future Aspirations:
- What would enhanced adaptability enable you to achieve in your personal and professional life?
- How does this align with your long-term goals?

Embracing the Journey Toward Enhanced Adaptability

As you progress through this guided self-assessment, remember that enhancing adaptability is a personal and dynamic journey. Embrace the process with openness and curiosity. The insights you gain will serve as a compass, guiding you toward:

- **Resilience:** Developing the capacity to bounce back from setbacks.
- **Growth:** Continuously learning and expanding your capabilities.
- **Success:** Achieving your goals in the face of change and uncertainty.

By actively engaging in self-reflection and targeted development, you empower yourself to navigate dynamic environments confidently and effectively. Your commitment to growth will not only benefit you but also inspire those around you to embrace change as an opportunity for collective advancement.

—

We've explored the multifaceted nature of thriving amidst flux. From understanding the dynamics of change and its psychological impact to developing a growth mindset and enhancing cognitive adaptability, each section has provided insights and strategies to navigate change effectively.

By shifting from reactive to proactive leadership, empowering your team, leveraging technology and innovation, and engaging in guided self-assessment, you are equipped with a comprehensive toolkit to lead confidently in dynamic environments.

Embrace the journey of continuous learning and adaptation. As you cultivate these skills and mindsets, you'll not only thrive amidst change but also inspire others to do the same, fostering a culture of resilience and innovation within your organization.

Remember: Change is inevitable, but growth is a choice. By choosing to enhance your adaptability, you're positioning yourself to navigate whatever the future holds with confidence and grace.

Setting Personalized Goals for Enhancing Adaptability

- "Personalized goals are the milestones on the journey of adaptability; they provide direction and purpose, ensuring continuous growth and resilience."

In the journey toward becoming more adaptable, setting personalized goals is a critical step. Clear and attainable objectives provide direction, while detailed implementation plans serve as the roadmap guiding you toward enhanced resilience and agility. This section will help you define specific goals tailored to your unique circumstances and outline actionable steps to achieve them.

Defining Clear and Attainable Objectives

Setting well-defined goals is foundational for personal growth and development. In the context of enhancing adaptability, goals help you focus your efforts on specific areas that will most effectively increase your capacity to navigate change.

Benefits of Clear Goals:
- **Direction:** Provide a clear path forward.
- **Motivation:** Inspire action and perseverance.
- **Measurement:** Enable tracking progress and celebrating milestones.
- **Accountability:** Encourage commitment to your development plan.

Introducing the WISE Framework for Goal-Setting

William Stanek's WISE framework—standing for Well-Defined, Inspiring, Sustainable, and Empowering—is a modern approach to goal-setting that emphasizes clarity, motivation, longevity, and personal growth. It is designed to guide individuals on their leadership and personal development journeys by aligning goals with their core values and long-term aspirations.

Components of the WISE Framework

1. Well-Defined

Description: Goals should be clear, precise, and unambiguous. They need to specify the who, what, when, where, and why to eliminate confusion and provide a clear path forward.

Implementation: Break down the goal into specific actions and measurable outcomes. Include deadlines and relevant details to maintain focus.

Example: Instead of saying, "Improve leadership skills," specify, "Attend three leadership workshops in the next six months focusing on communication, conflict resolution, and decision-making."

2. Inspiring

Description: Goals should ignite passion and enthusiasm. They need to resonate deeply with your personal values and aspirations to maintain motivation over time.

Implementation: Align goals with what genuinely matters to you. Visualize the positive impact achieving the goal will have on your life and others.

Example: "Become a mentor to junior team members to help them develop their leadership potential," which not only advances your skills but also contributes positively to others.

3. Sustainable

Description: Goals should be achievable over the long term without causing burnout or neglecting other important areas of life. They should fit within your available resources and time.

Implementation: Assess your current commitments and resources. Ensure the goal is realistic and can be integrated smoothly into your life.

Example: Allocate two hours every week for leadership skill development activities, balancing it with work and personal life.

4. Empowering

Description: Goals should boost your confidence and sense of agency. They should enable you to take control of your development and recognize your ability to effect change.

Implementation: Set goals that challenge you and require you to step out of your comfort zone. Take ownership of your progress and celebrate achievements along the way.

Example: "Lead a cross-functional project to improve team collaboration," which empowers you to make significant contributions and develop leadership skills.

Comparing WISE with SMART

While the SMART framework (Specific, Measurable, Achievable, Relevant, Time-bound) focuses on creating clear and trackable goals, the WISE framework adds an emotional and sustainable dimension to goal-setting.

- **Well-Defined vs. Specific:** Both emphasize clarity, but "Well-Defined" also encourages understanding the purpose behind the goal.
- **Inspiring vs. Relevant:** "Inspiring" goes deeper than "Relevant" by focusing on personal passion and motivation rather than just alignment with broader objectives.
- **Sustainable vs. Achievable:** "Sustainable" considers long-term feasibility and balance with other life aspects, whereas "Achievable" focuses on the attainability of the goal.
- **Empowering vs. Time-bound:** "Empowering" centers on personal growth and agency, while "Time-bound" emphasizes deadlines to create urgency.

Example of a WISE Goal

Non-WISE Goal: "I want to get better at public speaking."

WISE Goal: "Enroll in a public speaking course, practice delivering one presentation per week, and track progress using audience engagement and feedback metrics. Within six months, confidently deliver a 15-minute presentation to a large audience."

- **Well-Defined:** Specifies enrolling in a course, practicing weekly, and delivering a presentation within six months.
- **Inspiring:** Aims to build confidence and engage audiences, which can be highly motivating.
- **Sustainable:** Practicing once a week is a manageable commitment.
- **Empowering:** Focuses on building confidence and skill, empowering the individual to speak to large audiences.

Implementing the WISE Framework

1. Reflect on Your Values and Aspirations
- Identify what truly matters to you. This ensures your goals are inspiring and aligned with your long-term vision.

2. Assess Your Resources and Commitments
- Evaluate your time, energy, and resources to set sustainable goals that you can consistently work towards.

3. Break Down the Goal
- Divide your goal into smaller, manageable steps or milestones. This makes the goal well-defined and less overwhelming.

4. Monitor and Adjust
- Regularly review your progress and be open to adjusting your approach. This maintains the sustainability and empowering nature of your goal.

5. Celebrate Achievements
- Acknowledge and celebrate milestones reached. This reinforces your motivation and empowers you to continue progressing.

Benefits of the WISE Framework

- **Holistic Growth:** Encourages personal and professional development that is meaningful and sustainable.
- **Enhanced Motivation:** By setting inspiring goals, you maintain higher levels of enthusiasm and commitment.
- **Long-Term Success:** Sustainable goals prevent burnout and promote consistent progress over time.
- **Personal Empowerment:** Fosters a sense of control over your journey, boosting confidence and self-efficacy.

The WISE framework offers a comprehensive approach to goal-setting that not only focuses on the clarity and measurability of objectives but also deeply considers personal motivation, sustainability, and empowerment. By adopting the WISE principles, individuals can set goals that are more aligned with their true selves, leading to more fulfilling and lasting achievements.

Ready to Embrace the WISE Approach?

Consider revisiting your current goals and applying the WISE framework to them. Reflect on how each component—Well-Defined, Inspiring, Sustainable, Empowering—can enhance your objectives. This mindful approach can transform the way you set and achieve goals, paving the way for meaningful success in your leadership journey and personal development.

If you have specific goals you'd like to refine using the WISE framework or need further guidance on implementing these principles, feel free to share them, and we can work through the process together.

Identifying Key Areas for Development

Reflect on the self-assessment insights from the previous section to identify areas where enhancing adaptability will have the most significant impact. Consider focusing on:

- **Embracing Ambiguity:** Becoming comfortable with uncertainty and change.
- **Improving Decision-Making:** Enhancing your ability to make informed decisions quickly.
- **Fostering a Growth Mindset:** Adopting attitudes that support continuous learning.
- **Enhancing Emotional Resilience:** Building capacity to manage stress and recover from setbacks.
- **Strengthening Interpersonal Skills:** Improving communication and collaboration during transitions.

Aligning Objectives with Personal Aspirations

Ensure that your goals resonate with your values and long-term aspirations. This alignment increases motivation and the likelihood of sustained commitment.

Questions to Consider:
- How will enhancing adaptability contribute to your career progression?
- In what ways will increased adaptability improve your personal life?
- How does adaptability align with your core values and vision for the future?

Outlining Implementation Plans for Growth

Creating a Detailed Action Plan

An effective implementation plan translates your objectives into actionable steps. Consider the following components:

1. **Action Steps:** Specific activities you will undertake.
2. **Resources Needed:** Training, tools, or support required.
3. **Timeline:** Deadlines and milestones for each action.
4. **Success Metrics:** Indicators to measure progress.
5. **Accountability Mechanisms:** Methods to ensure you stay on track.

Action Plan Template:

Goal

- Improve emotional resilience by practicing mindfulness meditation daily.

Action Steps

- Research mindfulness techniques
- Set daily reminders
- Practice meditation for 10 minutes daily   - Meditation apps

Resources Needed

- Meditation Apps
- Quiet space

Timeline
- Start: [Date]
- End: [Date]

Success Metrics
- Daily meditation completed
- Reduced stress levels reported

Accountability
- Use habit-tracking app
- Weekly check-ins with mentor

Identifying Resources and Support

Consider what you need to achieve your goals:

- **Educational Materials:** Books, online courses, workshops.
- **Mentorship and Coaching:** Guidance from experienced individuals.
- **Technology Tools:** Apps for mindfulness, productivity, or learning.
- **Support Network:** Friends, family, or colleagues who can encourage you.

Monitoring Progress and Adjusting Plans

Regularly review your progress to stay aligned with your objectives:

- **Set Checkpoints:** Establish regular intervals (e.g., weekly, monthly) to assess progress.
- **Reflect on Learnings:** Identify what's working and what isn't.

- **Adjust as Needed:** Be flexible in modifying your plan to overcome obstacles or changing circumstances.

Anticipating Challenges and Developing Strategies

Prepare for potential obstacles:

Identify Potential Barriers:
- Time constraints
- Lack of resources
- Personal resistance to change

Develop Contingency Plans:
- Adjust timelines
- Seek alternative resources
- Engage in self-reflection to address resistance

Example:

Challenge: Difficulty maintaining daily meditation practice due to a busy schedule.

Strategy: Schedule meditation first thing in the morning or combine it with another routine activity.

Integrating the Holistic Intelligence Model

Leverage the 8 Pillars of the Holistic Intelligence Model to enrich your implementation plan:

1. Emotional Resilience (ER): Incorporate practices that enhance your ability to manage emotions, such as stress management techniques or emotional intelligence training.

2. Creative Intelligence (CrQ): Engage in activities that stimulate creativity, like brainstorming sessions or creative hobbies.

3. Practical Intelligence (PQ): Apply learned concepts to real-life situations through simulations or hands-on projects.

4. Cultural Intelligence (CQ): Expose yourself to diverse cultures through travel, language learning, or multicultural events.

5. Intrapersonal Intelligence:

- **Self-Reflection:** Maintain a journal to deepen self-awareness.
- **Mindfulness Practices:** Enhance self-regulation through meditation or yoga.

6. Interpersonal Intelligence:

- **Communication Skills:** Attend workshops on effective communication.
- **Networking:** Build relationships through professional groups or social events.

7. Ethical Intelligence (EthQ):

- **Ethics Training:** Participate in courses that explore ethical decision-making.
- **Volunteering:** Engage in community service to align actions with values.

8. Analytical Intelligence (AQ):

- **Critical Thinking Exercises:** Solve puzzles or case studies.
- **Data Analysis Skills:** Learn to interpret data relevant to your field.

Example Integration:

Goal: Enhance interpersonal intelligence to improve collaboration during change.

Action Steps:
- Enroll in a conflict resolution workshop (Interpersonal Intelligence).
- Practice active listening in daily conversations (Intrapersonal Intelligence).
- Participate in team-building activities (Emotional Resilience and Interpersonal Intelligence).

Practical Exercises and Tools

Exercise 1: Goal-Setting Worksheet

Use a structured worksheet to define your goals clearly.

Components:
- **Goal Statement:** What do you want to achieve?
- **Motivation:** Why is this goal important to you?
- **Alignment:** How does it align with your values and aspirations?
- **WISE Criteria:** Ensure the goal meets all WISE elements.
- **Potential Obstacles:** Identify challenges you may face.
- **Support Required:** Determine who or what can assist you.

Exercise 2: Action Plan Development

Create a detailed action plan using the template provided earlier. Break down each goal into manageable steps.

Exercise 3: Accountability Partner

Purpose: Increase commitment by involving someone else in your journey.

Instructions:
- Choose a trusted colleague, friend, or mentor.
- Share your goals and action plans.
- Schedule regular check-ins to discuss progress and challenges.

Exercise 4: Visualization and Affirmations

Visualization:
- Imagine yourself successfully adapting to change and achieving your goals.
- Visualize overcoming obstacles with confidence.

Affirmations:
- Create positive statements that reinforce your commitment (e.g., "I am adaptable and embrace change with enthusiasm").
- Repeat them daily to strengthen your mindset.

Reflection Questions

1. Clarity of Objectives:
- Are your goals specific and well-defined?

- Do they genuinely reflect your desires and motivations?

2. Feasibility:
- Are your goals achievable within the set timeframe?
- Do you have the necessary resources or know where to obtain them?

3. Action Plan Robustness:
- Does your plan include clear steps and timelines?
- Have you identified potential obstacles and strategies to address them?

4. Support Systems:
- Who can you turn to for encouragement and advice?
- How can you expand your support network?

5. Commitment Level:
- On a scale of 1 to 10, how committed are you to achieving these goals?
- What can you do to increase your commitment level?

Case Study: Transforming Adaptability Through Goal Setting

Background

Maria, a mid-level manager at a technology firm, realized that her reluctance to embrace new processes was hindering her career progression. She decided to enhance her adaptability.

Maria's Goal-Setting Process

1. Defining Objectives:
- **Goal:** Increase adaptability by embracing new technologies and processes within six months.
- **Specificity:** Focused on mastering two new project management tools.

2. Creating an Action Plan:
- **Action Steps:**
- Attend training sessions on the new tools.
- Apply the tools in managing a small project.
- Seek feedback from peers and supervisors.
- **Resources Needed:**
- Company-sponsored training.
- Access to software.
- Time allocated for learning.

3. Implementation:
- **Timeline:** Set milestones for completing training and implementing tools.
- **Monitoring Progress:** Regular check-ins with her supervisor.
- **Adjustments:** Addressed initial frustrations by joining a user group for additional support.

4. Outcome:
- Successfully integrated new tools into her workflow.
- Received positive feedback for improved efficiency.
- Enhanced her reputation as a proactive and adaptable leader.

Lessons Learned
- **Importance of Clear Goals:** Specific objectives provided direction.
- **Value of Support:** Seeking feedback and joining a user group offered encouragement and resources.
- **Adaptability Growth:** By setting and achieving her goals, Maria increased her confidence in navigating change.

Embracing Continuous Growth

Remember that enhancing adaptability is an ongoing process. As you achieve your initial goals, revisit and set new ones to continue your development journey. Stay open to learning and remain flexible in adapting your plans as you evolve.

Tips for Sustained Growth:
- **Celebrate Milestones:** Acknowledge your achievements to stay motivated.
- **Reflect Regularly:** Periodically assess your adaptability and identify new growth areas.
- **Stay Curious:** Seek out new experiences that challenge and expand your comfort zone.
- **Mentor Others:** Sharing your journey can reinforce your learning and inspire others.

By setting personalized goals and outlining detailed implementation plans, you take proactive control of your adaptability journey. This structured approach transforms aspirations into actionable steps, empowering you to navigate change with confidence and resilience.

As you move forward:

- **Stay Committed:** Keep your objectives in focus and maintain momentum.
- **Be Patient:** Personal growth takes time—allow yourself grace during setbacks.
- **Seek Support:** Leverage your network and resources to enhance your journey.
- **Embrace Change:** View each new challenge as an opportunity to apply and refine your adaptability skills.

Through deliberate effort and continuous learning, you'll develop the agility to thrive in dynamic environments, positioning yourself for sustained success in both your personal and professional life.

Remember: Adaptability is not a destination but a continuous journey of growth. Embrace the process, stay open to new experiences, and continue to cultivate the skills that will enable you to navigate the ever-changing landscapes of life and work successfully.

Case Study 2: The Adaptive Leader in Action

- "An adaptive leader not only survives change but leverages it to forge new paths, inspiring their team to achieve beyond the imaginable."

Antoine Girard, a seasoned professional in the pharmaceutical industry, assumed the role of Chief Scientific Officer (CSO) with a vision to revolutionize drug development. With a background in molecular biology and a track record of groundbreaking discoveries, Girard brought a wealth of scientific expertise to his leadership position. His leadership style is characterized by a unique blend of analytical rigor, strategic foresight, and a profound understanding of the rapidly evolving pharmaceutical landscape.

Girard's journey began in the research labs, where he made significant contributions to the understanding of cellular mechanisms in disease progression. His innovative approaches led to the development of several groundbreaking therapies, earning him recognition within the scientific community. This early success positioned Girard as a rising star in the industry, and he was soon entrusted with leadership roles.

Navigating Turbulent Waters: The Pharmaceutical Industry in Flux

Upon assuming the role of CSO, Girard faced a pharmaceutical landscape undergoing unprecedented change. Shifting regulatory landscapes, emerging technologies, and evolving patient expectations presented both opportunities and challenges. The industry demanded leaders who could not only navigate this turbulence but also drive innovation amidst uncertainty.

Embracing Disruption: Girard's Adaptive Leadership Approach

Girard's adaptive leadership approach was instrumental in steering the organization through these turbulent times. He recognized the need for agility and foresight, and he set out to create a culture that embraced change as an inherent part of progress. By fostering a mindset of continuous learning and adaptation, Girard instilled resilience and confidence in his team.

Agile Decision-Making: A Cornerstone of Girard's Leadership

One of Girard's most notable traits was his ability to make agile, data-driven decisions. He understood the value of gathering diverse perspectives, leveraging cross-functional expertise, and quickly synthesizing information to arrive at well-informed choices. This proficiency in decision-making became a cornerstone of his adaptive leadership style.

Cultivating a Culture of Innovation

Under Girard's guidance, the organization underwent a cultural shift towards innovation. He championed initiatives that encouraged creativity, experimentation, and calculated risk-taking. Girard believed that embracing uncertainty was the catalyst for transformative breakthroughs, and he actively sought out opportunities for disruptive innovation.

Strengthening Stakeholder Relationships

In a rapidly changing industry, Girard recognized the importance of building and nurturing strong relationships with stakeholders. He engaged in open dialogue with regulatory bodies, collaborated closely with research partners, and actively sought feedback from healthcare providers and patients. This collaborative approach not only fostered trust but also ensured that the organization remained aligned with the evolving needs of the healthcare ecosystem.

The Resilience Test: Navigating Unforeseen Challenges

During Girard's tenure, the industry faced unforeseen challenges, including regulatory shifts and unexpected clinical trial results. In these moments, Girard's adaptive leadership style truly shone. He remained composed under pressure, leveraging his analytical prowess to swiftly assess the situation and chart a new course forward.

Transformative Outcomes: Girard's Impact on Drug Development

Girard's tenure as CSO resulted in a series of transformative advancements in drug development. His emphasis on adaptive strategies led to the accelerated discovery and approval of several life-saving therapies. These achievements not only bolstered the organization's reputation but also positively impacted countless lives around the world.

Leaving a Legacy of Adaptability and Innovation

As Girard's time as CSO drew to a close, his legacy of adaptive leadership remained ingrained in the organization's DNA. The culture of innovation and resilience he fostered continued to drive progress, ensuring that the organization was well-equipped to navigate whatever changes lay ahead.

Antoine Girard's transformative impact as a Chief Scientific Officer exemplifies the power of adaptive leadership in the face of change and uncertainty. His ability to navigate complexity, drive innovation, and inspire resilience serves as a testament to the enduring influence of adaptive leadership in dynamic industries.

Analyzing Key Instances Demonstrating Adapting to Change and Uncertainty in Leadership

In this section, we will delve into key instances that showcase the transformative impact of adapting to change and uncertainty in leadership, drawing from real-world examples. One notable instance of adapting to change and uncertainty in leadership emerged in the tech sector, where a renowned CEO faced the challenge of rapidly evolving consumer demands and technological advancements. Recognizing the imperative to stay at the forefront of innovation, the CEO initiated a company-wide transformation focused on agility and adaptability. This shift in approach led to the development of cutting-edge products and services, enabling the company to maintain its competitive edge in an ever-changing market.

Navigating Regulatory Shifts in Healthcare

In the healthcare industry, a healthcare executive took on the formidable task of leading a large hospital network through a period of significant regulatory upheaval. Faced with new legislation and changing reimbursement models, the executive implemented a strategic pivot towards value-based care. By proactively aligning the organization with evolving regulatory requirements and emphasizing outcomes-driven healthcare delivery, the executive not only ensured compliance but also positioned the network as a leader in the shifting healthcare landscape.

Transforming a Legacy Brand in Retail

A seasoned retail leader faced the challenge of revitalizing a well-established, yet struggling, legacy brand in a rapidly changing consumer landscape. Recognizing the need for a strategic overhaul, the leader spearheaded a comprehensive rebranding effort, incorporating digital innovation and customer-centricity as core principles. This transformation not only revitalized the brand's image but also repositioned it as a dynamic player in the evolving retail industry.

Responding to Global Disruptions in Manufacturing

A manufacturing executive found themselves at the helm of a company grappling with the far-reaching impacts of a global crisis. Faced with supply chain disruptions, workforce challenges, and shifting customer demands, the executive orchestrated a swift and coordinated response. By diversifying supply chain sources, implementing flexible production processes, and prioritizing employee well-being, the executive guided the organization through the crisis and positioned it for long-term resilience.

Embracing Technological Disruption in Finance

In the financial sector, a forward-thinking leader navigated the wave of technological disruption sweeping through the industry. Recognizing the potential of fintech innovation, the leader initiated strategic partnerships and investments in emerging technologies. This forward-looking approach not only allowed the organization to stay ahead of the curve but also positioned it as a leader in the era of digital finance.

Pivoting to Remote Work in Response to a Global Pandemic

The onset of a global pandemic presented an unprecedented challenge for leaders across industries. A visionary CEO swiftly mobilized their organization to adapt to a remote work model, implementing robust technology infrastructure and virtual collaboration tools. By prioritizing employee well-being and maintaining a culture of transparency and open communication, the CEO not only ensured business continuity but also paved the way for a future of hybrid work models.

These key instances highlight the pivotal role of adapting to change and uncertainty in leadership. In each case, leaders demonstrated the ability to navigate complex challenges, seize opportunities, and drive transformative outcomes through their adaptive approach. These real-world examples serve as powerful illustrations of the enduring impact that adaptive leadership can have in dynamic and unpredictable environments.

Extracting Insights and Strategies from the Case Study

In this section, we will extract valuable insights and strategies from the case study of Antoine Girard, the Chief Scientific Officer (CSO) for the pharmaceutical industry. His exemplary leadership in adapting to change and uncertainty offers valuable lessons for leaders facing dynamic and unpredictable environments.

Embracing a Culture of Continuous Learning

One of the key takeaways from Antoine Girard's leadership is his emphasis on fostering a culture of continuous learning within his organization. He recognized that in a rapidly evolving industry like pharmaceuticals, staying at the forefront of scientific advancements was paramount. By encouraging his team to engage in ongoing education, attend industry conferences, and participate in collaborative research initiatives, Girard ensured that his organization remained agile and adaptable to emerging trends and technologies.

Prioritizing Cross-Functional Collaboration

Antoine Girard demonstrated the critical importance of cross-functional collaboration in navigating change and uncertainty. He broke down silos between research, development, regulatory affairs, and marketing departments, fostering a collaborative environment where diverse perspectives could converge. This approach enabled the organization to streamline decision-making processes, respond swiftly to market shifts, and develop innovative solutions that addressed evolving healthcare needs.

Cultivating a Growth Mindset

Girard's leadership style was characterized by a growth mindset, which he instilled in his team members. He encouraged them to view challenges as opportunities for growth and learning. By reframing setbacks as valuable learning experiences, he created a culture of resilience and adaptability. This mindset shift empowered his team to approach change with confidence and creativity, driving innovation even in the face of uncertainty.

Leveraging Technology as an Enabler

In an industry marked by rapid technological advancements, Antoine Girard recognized the transformative potential of leveraging cutting-edge technologies. He invested strategically in research and development initiatives focused on digital health, precision medicine, and artificial intelligence. This technological agility not only enhanced the organization's research capabilities but also positioned it as a pioneer in harnessing the power of data-driven healthcare solutions.

Proactive Scenario Planning and Risk Mitigation

Girard demonstrated a proactive approach to scenario planning and risk mitigation. He encouraged his team to anticipate potential disruptions, whether they stemmed from regulatory changes, supply chain vulnerabilities, or emerging competitive threats. By conducting thorough risk assessments and developing contingency plans, the organization was better prepared to navigate uncertainties and maintain operational continuity.

Embracing Agile Decision-Making Processes

Antoine Girard emphasized the importance of agile decision-making processes in a rapidly evolving industry. He implemented frameworks that enabled the organization to make informed decisions swiftly, without sacrificing thorough analysis. This nimble approach allowed the organization to capitalize on emerging opportunities and pivot quickly in response to market dynamics.

Nurturing a Culture of Adaptability

Girard's leadership style fostered a culture of adaptability and flexibility. He encouraged his team members to be open to change and to embrace new approaches to problem-solving. This cultural shift empowered employees at all levels to contribute innovative ideas and solutions, ensuring that the organization remained agile and responsive in a constantly changing landscape.

Balancing Short-Term Goals with Long-Term Vision

While navigating change and uncertainty, Antoine Girard struck a delicate balance between short-term goals and long-term strategic vision. He understood the need to deliver immediate results while also positioning the organization for sustainable growth and impact. This dual-focus approach ensured that the organization remained resilient in the face of immediate challenges while also preparing for future opportunities.

Fostering a Culture of Transparency and Communication

Effective communication was a cornerstone of Girard's leadership. He prioritized transparency and ensured that information flowed freely within the organization. This open communication culture built trust among team members and stakeholders, facilitating collaboration and alignment towards common goals. It also allowed for a more agile response to unexpected changes, as everyone was well-informed and empowered to make informed decisions.

Empowering Team Members through Autonomy

Antoine Girard empowered his team members by granting them a degree of autonomy and decision-making authority.

He understood that in an ever-changing environment, employees on the front lines often had the most relevant insights and expertise. By entrusting them with responsibilities and providing the necessary support, he tapped into their potential to drive innovation and adaptability.

Navigating Regulatory Complexity with Expertise

In the highly regulated pharmaceutical industry, Girard demonstrated a mastery of navigating complex regulatory landscapes. He established a dedicated regulatory affairs team and invested in their training and development. This expertise in compliance and regulatory affairs allowed the organization to respond swiftly and effectively to evolving industry standards, ensuring that their products met all necessary requirements.

Encouraging a Customer-Centric Approach

Antoine Girard prioritized a customer-centric approach, recognizing that understanding the needs and preferences of healthcare providers and patients was essential to success. He implemented initiatives to gather feedback, conduct market research, and engage with key stakeholders. This customer-centric focus allowed the organization to develop products and solutions that directly addressed the evolving demands of the healthcare ecosystem.

Building Resilience through Diversity and Inclusion

Girard understood the value of a diverse and inclusive workforce in building organizational resilience. He actively promoted diversity in hiring and leadership development, ensuring that the organization benefited from a wide range of perspectives and experiences. This diversity of thought and background proved invaluable in generating innovative solutions and navigating complex challenges.

Embracing Change as a Catalyst for Innovation

Antoine Girard viewed change not as a disruptive force, but as a catalyst for innovation. He encouraged his team members to embrace change as an opportunity for growth and creativity. By reframing change as a positive force for progress, he fostered a culture where individuals were motivated to seek out new solutions and approaches.

Leveraging Data-Driven Insights for Strategic Direction

In an era of data abundance, Girard recognized the transformative potential of harnessing data-driven insights. He championed the use of advanced analytics and data science to inform strategic decision-making. This evidence-based approach allowed the organization to make informed choices, respond swiftly to market trends, and develop targeted solutions that met the evolving needs of healthcare stakeholders.

Fostering a Growth-Oriented Mindset

Antoine Girard's leadership style was characterized by a growth-oriented mindset. He encouraged his team members to view challenges as opportunities for learning and development. This mindset shift empowered individuals to approach change with a positive outlook, driving a culture of resilience and adaptability.

Balancing Risk-Taking with Prudent Decision-Making

While Girard embraced innovation, he also recognized the importance of balancing risk-taking with prudent decision-making. He established robust processes for evaluating and mitigating risks associated with new initiatives. This balanced approach allowed the organization to pursue innovative solutions with confidence, knowing that risks were carefully considered and managed.

Navigating Ambiguity with Confidence

In an industry marked by scientific complexity and regulatory uncertainty, Antoine Girard demonstrated a remarkable ability to navigate ambiguity with confidence. He encouraged his team members to approach complex challenges with a structured yet flexible mindset. This enabled them to make informed decisions even in the absence of complete information, ensuring that the organization could adapt swiftly to evolving circumstances.

Instilling a Sense of Purpose and Mission

Girard understood the power of a compelling organizational mission in galvanizing teams during times of change and uncertainty. He articulated a clear sense of purpose that resonated with employees at all levels. This shared mission provided a unifying force, inspiring individuals to overcome challenges and work together towards a common goal.

Embracing Agility in Strategic Planning

Antoine Girard's strategic planning approach was characterized by a strong emphasis on agility. He recognized that in a rapidly evolving industry, long-term plans needed to be flexible and adaptable. He implemented iterative planning processes that allowed the organization to adjust strategies in response to emerging trends and unexpected developments.

Leading with Resilience and Optimism

Perhaps the most prominent insight from Antoine Girard's leadership style was his unwavering resilience and optimism. In the face of complex challenges and uncertainty, he remained a steady and optimistic presence. His positive outlook and confidence in the organization's ability to adapt were instrumental in rallying his team and maintaining morale during times of change.

Empowering Employees as Change Agents

Girard empowered employees at all levels to act as change agents within the organization. He provided opportunities for professional development, encouraged the pursuit of innovative ideas, and recognized and rewarded contributions to positive change. This approach not only enhanced individual growth but also created a culture where employees felt empowered to drive meaningful transformations.

Adapting to Feedback and Iterative Improvement

Antoine Girard placed a strong emphasis on feedback and iterative improvement. He established mechanisms for gathering input from team members and stakeholders, valuing their insights as critical drivers of organizational growth. This iterative approach to improvement allowed the organization to continuously adapt and refine its strategies in response to evolving circumstances.

Nurturing Resilient Leadership Succession

Antoine Girard recognized the importance of cultivating resilient leadership beyond his own tenure. He actively mentored and groomed emerging leaders within the organization, imparting the principles of adaptability and resilience. By ensuring a pipeline of leaders who embodied these qualities, he secured the organization's ability to navigate future uncertainties with confidence.

Balancing Innovation with Ethical Considerations

In an industry with profound societal impact, Antoine Girard was vigilant about balancing innovation with ethical considerations. He championed initiatives focused on responsible research and development, ensuring that the organization's advancements were aligned with ethical and moral imperatives. This commitment to ethical leadership set a standard for responsible innovation in the pharmaceutical sector.

Lessons in Adapting to Change and Uncertainty from Antoine Girard's Leadership Style

Antoine Girard's leadership style provides a wealth of lessons for leaders facing change and uncertainty in dynamic industries. His approach embodies adaptability, resilience, and a strategic orientation. Here are the key lessons that can be gleaned from Antoine Girard's leadership style:

1. Embrace Change as an Opportunity for Growth

Antoine Girard's leadership exemplifies the mindset that change, while often challenging, can be a powerful catalyst for growth and innovation. By reframing change as an opportunity rather than a threat, leaders can inspire their teams to approach challenges with a sense of curiosity and possibility.

2. Foster a Culture of Continuous Learning

Girard's emphasis on continuous learning is a cornerstone of his leadership style. He understands that in rapidly evolving industries, knowledge is a critical asset. Leaders can follow suit by creating an environment where ongoing education, skill development, and knowledge-sharing are valued and encouraged.

3. Prioritize Cross-Functional Collaboration

Antoine Girard recognized that the best solutions often emerge from diverse perspectives. By breaking down silos and fostering collaboration between different functions and teams, leaders can leverage the collective intelligence of their organization to navigate complex challenges and seize new opportunities.

4. Balance Risk-Taking with Prudent Decision-Making

Innovative leaders, like Girard, understand the importance of calculated risk-taking. By conducting thorough risk assessments and considering potential outcomes, leaders can strike a balance between seizing opportunities and ensuring that risks are managed effectively.

5. Leverage Technology as an Enabler

Antoine Girard's strategic investments in technology demonstrate the power of leveraging innovation to gain a competitive edge. Leaders can similarly drive organizational success by identifying and adopting cutting-edge technologies that align with their strategic goals and industry trends.

6. Nurture a Growth Mindset

Girard's emphasis on a growth mindset empowers individuals to view challenges as opportunities for learning and development. Leaders who foster this mindset within their teams create a culture of adaptability, where employees are more inclined to proactively seek out solutions and embrace change.

7. Navigate Regulatory Complexity with Expertise

In highly regulated industries, like pharmaceuticals, a deep understanding of regulatory affairs is essential. Leaders can emulate Girard's approach by investing in regulatory expertise and ensuring compliance with industry standards, allowing their organizations to navigate complex landscapes with confidence.

8. Maintain a Long-Term Strategic Vision

While adapting to immediate changes is crucial, Girard's leadership underscores the importance of balancing short-term tactics with a long-term strategic vision. Leaders should guide their organizations with an eye toward the future, ensuring that tactical decisions align with broader strategic objectives.

9. Empower Employees as Change Agents

Antoine Girard empowered his team members to act as change agents within the organization. Leaders can follow suit by providing opportunities for professional growth, encouraging the pursuit of innovative ideas, and recognizing and rewarding contributions to positive change.

10. Instill a Sense of Purpose and Mission

A clear sense of purpose is a powerful motivator, especially during times of change and uncertainty. Leaders can inspire their teams by articulating a compelling organizational mission that resonates with employees at all levels, providing a unifying force that drives collective efforts.

11. Adapt to Feedback and Iterative Improvement

Antoine Girard's commitment to feedback and iterative improvement highlights the importance of listening to team members and stakeholders. Leaders should actively seek input, value diverse perspectives, and use feedback as a catalyst for ongoing improvement and adaptation.

12. Foster Resilient Leadership Succession

Girard's foresight in grooming emerging leaders within the organization ensures continuity of resilient leadership. Leaders should invest in mentoring and developing future leaders, securing the organization's ability to navigate future uncertainties with confidence.

13. Balance Innovation with Ethical Considerations

In industries with far-reaching societal impact, ethical considerations should guide decision-making. Leaders can follow Girard's example by championing responsible practices, ensuring that innovation aligns with ethical and moral imperatives.

14. Lead with Resilience and Optimism

During times of change and uncertainty, a leader's resilience and optimism set the tone for the entire organization. By maintaining a positive outlook and a steady demeanor, leaders can inspire confidence and determination in their teams.

15. Empower Employees through Autonomy

Antoine Girard's empowerment of team members through autonomy allowed them to contribute their expertise effectively. Leaders who trust their employees and provide the necessary support create a culture of ownership and accountability, enabling the organization to adapt more efficiently.

16. Navigate Ambiguity with Confidence

In complex environments, leaders must navigate ambiguity with confidence. Antoine Girard's structured yet flexible approach to problem-solving serves as a model for making informed decisions even in uncertain circumstances.

17. Build Resilience through Diversity and Inclusion

A diverse and inclusive workforce enhances organizational resilience. Leaders should actively promote diversity and inclusion, recognizing that varied perspectives and experiences are valuable assets in navigating change and uncertainty.

18. Balance Short-Term Goals with Long-Term Vision

Leaders can learn from Girard's approach of balancing short-term objectives with a long-term strategic vision. This dual-focus approach ensures that the organization remains resilient in the face of immediate challenges while also preparing for future opportunities.

19. Encourage a Customer-Centric Approach

Understanding and meeting the needs of customers and stakeholders is paramount. Leaders can prioritize a customer-centric approach by actively seeking feedback, conducting market research, and engaging with key stakeholders to inform decision-making.

20. Embrace Agility in Strategic Planning

In rapidly evolving industries, strategic plans must be flexible and adaptable. Leaders can follow Girard's example by implementing iterative planning processes that allow the organization to adjust strategies in response to emerging trends and unexpected developments.

Incorporating these lessons into their own leadership styles, leaders can navigate change and uncertainty with confidence, inspiring their teams to adapt and thrive in dynamic environments. By drawing inspiration from Antoine Girard's exemplary leadership, they can chart a course of resilience, innovation, and sustained success.

These lessons drawn from Antoine Girard's leadership style are invaluable for leaders facing the challenges of change and uncertainty. They serve as a roadmap for navigating dynamic industries with resilience, strategic acumen, and a focus on long-term success. By embracing these principles, leaders can steer their organizations through turbulent times and emerge stronger, more adaptive, and better poised for the future.

Practical Takeaways for Leaders Adapting to Change and Uncertainty

Here are practical takeaways for leaders looking to adapt to change and uncertainty, inspired by Antoine Girard's exemplary leadership style:

1. Foster a Culture of Adaptability

Cultivate a workplace culture that values and encourages adaptability. Encourage employees to embrace change and view it as an opportunity for growth and learning.

2. Invest in Continuous Learning and Development

Provide opportunities for ongoing learning and skill development. Offer training programs, workshops, and access to resources that empower employees to acquire new skills and knowledge.

3. Facilitate Cross-Functional Collaboration

Break down silos within the organization and create spaces for different departments and teams to collaborate. Encourage the exchange of ideas and expertise to drive innovation and problem-solving.

4. Implement Agile Decision-Making Processes

Adopt agile decision-making frameworks that allow for rapid responses to changing circumstances. Empower teams to make decisions at the appropriate level, minimizing bureaucratic delays.

5. Stay Informed and Anticipate Trends

Stay abreast of industry trends, technological advancements, and regulatory changes. Anticipate shifts in the external environment and position the organization to capitalize on emerging opportunities.

6. Cultivate a Growth Mindset

Encourage employees to embrace challenges, learn from failures, and see setbacks as opportunities for improvement. Foster a growth mindset that promotes resilience and a willingness to adapt.

7. Emphasize the Importance of Regulatory Compliance

Ensure that the organization maintains a robust understanding of regulatory requirements and compliance standards. Prioritize adherence to industry-specific regulations to mitigate risks and ensure ethical operations.

8. Leverage Technology for Agility

Embrace technology solutions that enhance organizational agility. Implement systems that facilitate rapid communication, data analysis, and decision-making.

9. Encourage Employee-Led Innovation

Create channels for employees to contribute their innovative ideas and solutions. Recognize and reward creativity and entrepreneurship within the organization.

10. Establish Contingency Plans and Scenario Analyses

Develop contingency plans that outline responses to potential disruptions or crises. Conduct scenario analyses to prepare for a range of possible future scenarios.

11. Lead by Example

Demonstrate adaptability and a willingness to embrace change through your own actions and decisions. Serve as a role model for the behavior and mindset you wish to see in your team.

12. Communicate Transparently and Frequently

Keep employees informed about changes and developments within the organization. Provide context and rationale for decisions, and be open to feedback and questions.

13. Build a Diverse and Inclusive Workforce

Embrace diversity of thought, background, and experience within the organization. A diverse workforce brings a variety of perspectives that can be invaluable in navigating change.

14. Encourage Experimentation and Prototyping

Foster a culture of experimentation where teams are encouraged to test new ideas and approaches. Embrace a mindset of continuous improvement through iterative processes.

15. Establish Key Performance Indicators (KPIs) for Adaptability

Define and track metrics that measure the organization's ability to adapt to change. Use KPIs to assess the effectiveness of adaptability initiatives and identify areas for improvement.

16. Provide Resources for Well-Being and Resilience

Support employees in maintaining their physical, emotional, and mental well-being. Offer resources such as wellness programs, mental health support, and stress management techniques.

17. Encourage Networking and Industry Involvement

Facilitate opportunities for employees to network with peers, attend industry conferences, and participate in professional development activities. Exposure to external perspectives can enhance adaptability.

18. Celebrate Successes and Learn from Failures

Recognize and celebrate achievements, no matter how small. Similarly, view failures as learning opportunities and encourage a culture of reflection and continuous improvement.

19. Promote a Customer-Centric Approach

Prioritize understanding and meeting the needs of customers and stakeholders. Solicit feedback, conduct customer research, and align products and services with market demands.

20. Revisit and Revise Strategies Regularly

Regularly review and update organizational strategies in response to evolving circumstances. Ensure that the strategic direction remains aligned with the current environment and future opportunities.

By incorporating these practical takeaways into their leadership approach, leaders can effectively navigate change and uncertainty, driving their organizations towards sustained success. Inspired by Antoine Girard's adaptive leadership style, these strategies provide a roadmap for leaders seeking to thrive in dynamic and unpredictable environments.

Leadership Case Reviews: Mastering Situations in Adapting to Change and Uncertainty

Because the real world is where some of our most valuable lessons are learned, let's now look at instances that demonstrate that effective leadership in adapting to change and uncertainty requires a combination of strategic foresight, adaptability, and a deep understanding of the evolving landscape. These leaders not only recognized the need for change but also had the courage and acumen to navigate the complexities of transformation, ultimately positioning their organizations for long-term success.

Strategic Pivot in Tech Start-up

- **Analysis**   In the face of a rapidly changing market, the CEO of a tech start-up recognized the need for a strategic pivot. Instead of clinging to the original business model, the leader swiftly adapted to emerging trends and redirected the company towards a new, more promising niche. This bold move not only saved the company from potential failure but also positioned it as a frontrunner in the evolving industry.
- **Lesson**   This instance underscores the significance of audacious decision-making in swiftly adapting to emerging trends. Leaders should be prepared to pivot strategically when the circumstances demand, even if it means redirecting the company towards a new and more promising niche.

Global Expansion in Manufacturing

- **Analysis**   A seasoned manufacturing executive led a successful global expansion initiative. Understanding the shifting demographics and market demands, the leader navigated complex international regulations, cultural nuances, and supply chain challenges. Through careful planning and strategic partnerships, the company not only expanded its footprint but also gained a competitive edge in the global market.
- **Lesson**   This key instance underscores the importance of strategic planning and informed partnerships in global expansions. It highlights the competitive advantage gained by understanding and addressing the unique challenges of international markets.

Transformation of a Traditional Institution:

- **Analysis**   The head of a long-standing educational institution faced the challenge of adapting to a rapidly changing educational landscape. Instead of resisting change, the leader embraced innovation, introducing technology-driven learning methods and flexible curriculum structures. This transformation not only ensured the institution's relevance but also positioned it as a pioneer in modern education.
- **Lesson**   This instance emphasizes the necessity of embracing change and leveraging innovation to stay relevant. Leaders in traditional sectors should be willing to adapt and introduce progressive approaches to secure their institutions' position in a dynamic environment.

Crisis Management in Healthcare

- **Analysis**   A healthcare administrator faced a sudden influx of patients during a public health crisis. The leader

demonstrated exceptional crisis management skills by swiftly reallocating resources, mobilizing additional staff, and implementing new protocols. This not only ensured the well-being of patients but also garnered praise for the organization's effective response to the crisis.
- **Lesson** This instance highlights the critical importance of effective crisis management in healthcare leadership. It emphasizes the need for leaders to possess the agility and decision-making capacity to respond swiftly and decisively in high-pressure situations.

Market Expansion in Retail

- **Analysis** The CEO of a retail chain recognized the need to diversify and expand into new markets to stay ahead of evolving consumer preferences. Through meticulous market research, the leader identified untapped opportunities and led the company's successful entry into new regions. This strategic expansion not only boosted revenue but also solidified the company's position as an industry leader.
- **Lesson** This key instance emphasizes the strategic significance of market research and expansion for sustainable growth. It underscores the advantages of proactively identifying and capitalizing on emerging market trends.

Innovation in a Research Institution

- **Analysis** The director of a research institution faced the challenge of maintaining relevance in a rapidly evolving scientific landscape. By fostering a culture of curiosity, encouraging interdisciplinary collaboration, and investing in cutting-edge technologies, the leader propelled the institution to the forefront of scientific discovery. This not

only attracted top talent but also secured substantial research grants and partnerships.
- **Lesson** This instance underscores the critical role of fostering a culture of innovation in research institutions. It highlights the impact of visionary leadership in attracting talent and securing substantial research grants.

Turnaround in a Financial Institution

- **Analysis** The CEO of a struggling financial institution executed a remarkable turnaround. By conducting a thorough analysis of market trends and customer needs, the leader implemented a series of strategic initiatives, including streamlined operations, enhanced customer service, and innovative product offerings. This transformation not only restored profitability but also rebuilt trust with stakeholders.
- **Lesson** This instance showcases the transformative power of customer-centric initiatives and strategic planning in the financial sector. It emphasizes the capacity of leaders to identify and implement tailored solutions for organizational revival.

Adapting to Regulatory Changes in Pharmaceuticals

- **Analysis** The head of a pharmaceutical company navigated a complex landscape of evolving regulations and compliance requirements. By assembling a dedicated regulatory team, closely monitoring policy changes, and proactively adjusting operational practices, the leader ensured the company remained compliant while continuing to bring innovative products to market.
- **Lesson** This key instance underscores the criticality of regulatory acumen and adaptability in the pharmaceutical industry. It highlights the significance of robust regulatory

strategies in enabling the continued success of companies within a highly regulated sector.

Cultural Transformation in a Large Corporation

- **Analysis**   The CEO of a multinational corporation recognized the need for a cultural shift to foster innovation and agility. Through transparent communication, targeted training programs, and the implementation of flexible work arrangements, the leader successfully transformed the company's culture. This shift not only improved employee morale and productivity but also led to a surge in innovative solutions.
- **Lesson**   This instance demonstrates the profound impact of cultural transformation on organizational dynamics and performance. It emphasizes the pivotal role of leadership in driving cultural change to foster innovation and adaptability.

E-commerce Disruption in Retail

- **Analysis**   Faced with the rise of e-commerce giants, the leader of a traditional retail chain orchestrated a digital transformation. By investing in an online presence, optimizing the customer experience, and leveraging data analytics, the company successfully transitioned into the digital age. This strategic move not only retained existing customers but also attracted a new generation of tech-savvy consumers.
- **Lesson**   This key instance highlights the strategic imperative for traditional retailers to adapt to the digital landscape. It underscores the benefits of embracing technology and data-driven strategies to remain competitive in the evolving retail industry.

These key instances collectively illuminate the diverse facets of effective leadership in navigating change and uncertainty. They serve as powerful examples of the strategic foresight, adaptability, and innovative thinking that distinguish exceptional leaders in dynamic environments. Each instance offers unique lessons that aspiring and experienced leaders can draw upon to enhance their own leadership effectiveness.

The Ongoing Journey of Adaptability in Leadership

- *"Adaptability is not a destination but a perpetual voyage; leaders who embrace this journey transform challenges into stepping stones for lasting success."*

In the ever-evolving landscape of modern business, adaptability is not a destination but a continuous journey. Leaders who view change not as a disruptive force but as a catalyst for growth and innovation position themselves and their organizations to thrive amid uncertainty. This section delves into the profound significance of embracing change and provides strategies to foster a culture of innovation that propels organizations to new heights.

Embracing Change as a Catalyst for Growth

Change is often accompanied by feelings of uncertainty and discomfort. However, visionary leaders recognize that within every change lies the seed of opportunity. By reframing change as a positive force, leaders can:

- **Uncover Hidden Potentials:** Challenges presented by change often reveal latent talents and capabilities within individuals and teams.
- **Develop New Skills:** Navigating new terrains necessitates learning and growth, enhancing personal and professional competencies.

- **Expand Capacities:** Adapting to change enhances an organization's ability to handle future uncertainties with greater ease.

Key Principles:
- **1. Adopt a Growth Mindset:** Embrace the belief that abilities and intelligence can be developed through dedication and hard work. This mindset fosters a love of learning and resilience essential for great accomplishment.
- **2. View Challenges as Opportunities:** Recognize that obstacles are not barriers but stepping stones to innovation and improvement.
- **3. Embrace Continuous Learning:** Cultivate a culture where learning is ongoing, and knowledge is shared openly.

Change disrupts the status quo, prompting leaders and organizations to:

- **Think Creatively:** Seek novel solutions to emerging problems.
- **Explore Uncharted Territories:** Venture into new markets or adopt innovative technologies.
- **Enhance Competitiveness:** Stay ahead of industry trends and outpace competitors.

Case Study: Netflix's Transformation

Background:

Initial Model: Netflix began as a DVD rental service, competing with established entities like Blockbuster.

Embracing Change: Recognizing the shift in consumer preferences toward digital content, Netflix invested in streaming technology.

Actions Taken:

Innovated Delivery Model: Transitioned from physical DVDs to an online streaming platform.

Original Content Creation: Began producing original content to differentiate itself and add value.

Outcomes:

Market Leadership: Became a dominant player in the entertainment industry.

Continuous Growth: Adapted to changing consumer behaviors, leading to sustained success.

Lessons Learned:

Proactive Adaptation: Anticipating industry shifts allowed Netflix to capitalize on emerging trends.

Innovation Culture: Embracing change fostered an environment where innovation thrived.

Fostering a Culture of Innovation

Leaders set the tone for organizational culture. By championing innovation, they encourage teams to:

- **Experiment:** Try new ideas without fear of failure.

- **Collaborate:** Share knowledge and work together to solve complex problems.
- **Take Calculated Risks:** Assess potential rewards against risks to make informed decisions.

Strategies for Leaders:

1. Encourage Open Communication:

- **Idea Sharing Platforms:** Implement systems where employees can propose ideas and provide feedback.
- **Transparent Dialogue:** Foster an environment where questions and discussions are welcomed.

2. Provide Resources and Support:

- **Invest in Training:** Offer learning opportunities to develop innovative skills.
- **Allocate Time for Innovation:** Allow employees dedicated time to work on creative projects (e.g., Google's "20% time" policy).

3. Recognize and Reward Innovation:

- **Celebrate Successes:** Acknowledge achievements publicly to motivate others.
- **Learn from Failures:** Analyze unsuccessful attempts to extract valuable lessons.

Creating an Environment Conducive to Experimentation

Implementing Processes:

- **Agile Methodologies:** Adopt flexible approaches that allow for rapid prototyping and iteration.

- **Cross-Functional Teams:** Bring together diverse perspectives to enhance creativity.

Cultivating Psychological Safety:

- **No-Blame Culture:** Encourage risk-taking by ensuring employees are not punished for failures.
- **Empathy and Support:** Leaders should show understanding and provide assistance when challenges arise.

Case Study: 3M's Innovation Ecosystem

Background:

- **Innovation Legacy:** 3M is known for creating products like Post-it Notes and Scotch Tape.

Actions Taken:

- **15% Rule:** Allowed employees to use 15% of their time on projects of their choosing.
- **Cross-Pollination:** Encouraged collaboration across departments.

Outcomes:

- **Product Diversity:** Over 60,000 products developed, contributing to consistent growth.
- **Employee Engagement:** High levels of motivation and job satisfaction.

Lessons Learned:

- **Empowerment:** Giving employees autonomy fuels creativity.
- **Resource Allocation:** Investing in innovation yields long-term dividends.

Integrating the Holistic Intelligence Model

Embracing change and fostering innovation align with the Holistic Intelligence Model's pillars:

1. **Creative Intelligence (CrQ):** Encourages thinking outside the box and generating novel ideas.

2. **Emotional Resilience (ER):** Supports individuals in managing the uncertainties of change.

3. **Analytical Intelligence (AQ):** Enables critical evaluation of new ideas and strategic implementation.

4. **Practical Intelligence (PQ):** Facilitates the application of innovative concepts in real-world settings.

5. **Intrapersonal Intelligence:** Enhances self-awareness, allowing leaders to recognize their attitudes toward change and innovation.

6. **Interpersonal Intelligence:** Strengthens relationships and communication, vital for collaborative innovation.

7. **Cultural Intelligence (CQ):** Promotes inclusivity and leverages diverse perspectives in innovation processes.

8. **Ethical Intelligence (EthQ):** Ensures that innovation aligns with ethical standards and societal values.

Practical Strategies and Exercises

Exercise 1: Innovation Challenge

Purpose: Stimulate creative thinking and problem-solving within your team.

Steps:

1. **Identify a Challenge:** Select a current issue or opportunity within the organization.

2. **Form Diverse Teams:** Assemble groups with varied skills and backgrounds.

3. **Set Parameters:** Provide guidelines but encourage freedom in approach.

4. **Allocate Time:** Dedicate time for teams to develop and prototype solutions.

5. **Present Solutions:** Have teams share their ideas with leadership and peers.

6. **Implement and Iterate:** Support the implementation of viable solutions and allow for refinements.

Exercise 2: Reflection on Change

Purpose: Enhance personal understanding of change as a growth catalyst.

Instructions:

1. **Reflect on Past Changes:** Identify significant changes you've experienced.

2. **Analyze Outcomes:** Consider how these changes led to personal or professional growth.

3. **Identify Lessons Learned:** Extract insights that can inform future approaches to change.

4. **Set Intentions:** Determine how you will embrace change proactively moving forward.

Exercise 3: Building an Innovation Toolkit

Purpose: Equip yourself and your team with methods to foster innovation.

Components to Include:

- **Brainstorming Techniques:** Mind mapping, GROW analysis, or the Six Thinking Hats method.
- **Design Thinking Framework:** Empathize, define, ideate, prototype, and test.
- **Collaboration Tools:** Utilize software that facilitates teamwork and idea sharing.

Reflection Questions

1. **Personal Attitudes Toward Change:**

- How do you typically react to change in your personal and professional life?

- What beliefs do you hold about change that may limit or enhance your adaptability?

2. **Leadership Practices:**

- In what ways do you currently foster a culture of innovation within your team?
- How can you more effectively encourage experimentation and learning from failures?

3. **Organizational Culture:**

- Does your organization's culture support or hinder innovation?
- What steps can you take to influence positive cultural shifts toward embracing change?

Additional Insights

Research Findings

Innovation and Performance: Organizations that prioritize innovation tend to outperform their peers, demonstrating higher growth rates and profitability (Boston Consulting Group).

Employee Engagement: Companies with cultures that encourage innovation report higher levels of employee engagement and satisfaction (Gallup).

Quotes to Inspire
- **Winston Churchill:** "To improve is to change; to be perfect is to change often."

- **Charles Darwin:** "It is not the strongest or the most intelligent who will survive but those who can best manage change."
- **Peter Drucker:** "The greatest danger in times of turbulence is not the turbulence—it is to act with yesterday's logic."

—

Viewing change as a catalyst for growth and innovation transforms the challenges of uncertainty into opportunities for advancement. Leaders who embrace this mindset not only adapt to evolving circumstances but also inspire their teams to innovate and excel. By fostering a culture that values creativity, experimentation, and continuous learning, organizations can navigate the complexities of the modern business environment with confidence and agility.

Embracing change requires courage, vision, and a commitment to personal and collective growth. As you continue on this ongoing journey of adaptability in leadership, remember that each step taken to welcome change is a step toward unlocking new potentials and achieving greater heights of success.

Change is inevitable, but how we respond to it defines our leadership and the trajectory of our organizations. By embracing change as an ally rather than an adversary, we open doors to innovation, growth, and endless possibilities. Let us commit to viewing change through a lens of opportunity, fostering cultures where innovation thrives, and leading with vision and adaptability into the future.

Tools and Techniques for Adapting to Change and Uncertainty in Leadership

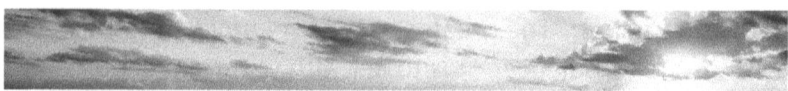

- *"Equipped with the right tools and techniques, leaders can turn the unpredictable currents of change into opportunities for strategic advantage."*

In an era characterized by rapid change and unprecedented uncertainty, leaders must equip themselves with a robust toolkit of strategies and methodologies to navigate the complexities of the modern business landscape effectively. This section explores a comprehensive array of tools and techniques designed to enhance adaptability, foster resilience, and drive innovation within organizations. By leveraging these approaches, leaders can anticipate challenges, respond proactively, and turn uncertainties into opportunities for growth.

1. Scenario Planning

Anticipating Future Possibilities

Definition: Scenario planning is a strategic tool that enables leaders to envision and prepare for a range of potential future situations. By considering various plausible scenarios, organizations can develop flexible strategies to navigate uncertainties.

Key Steps:

1. **Identify Driving Forces:** Analyze external factors such as economic trends, technological advancements, regulatory changes, and social dynamics that could impact the organization.

2. **Develop Scenarios:** Create detailed narratives for different future states, including best-case, worst-case, and alternative scenarios.

3. **Analyze Implications:** Assess the potential impact of each scenario on organizational objectives, operations, and stakeholders.

4. **Formulate Strategies:** Develop action plans and contingency measures tailored to each scenario.

5. **Monitor Indicators:** Establish key signals that may indicate which scenario is unfolding to adjust strategies promptly.

Case Study: Royal Dutch Shell

Background: In the 1970s, Shell used scenario planning to anticipate oil price fluctuations.

Outcome: By preparing for possible scenarios, Shell navigated the oil crisis more effectively than competitors, securing a stronger market position.

Practical Exercise:

Scenario Planning Workshop: Assemble a cross-functional team to conduct a scenario planning exercise focusing on a critical aspect of your business.

2. WISE Model

Structured Coaching for Development

Definition: The WISE (Well-Defined, Inspiring, Sustainable, and Empowering) is a coaching framework used to guide individuals and teams through problem-solving and goal-setting processes.

Key Components:
- Define clear, specific objectives.
- Assess the current situation, identifying challenges and resources.
- Explore possible strategies and solutions.
- Commit to action steps and establish accountability.

Application in Leadership:

Personal Development: Leaders use WISE to enhance their adaptability by setting personal goals for growth.

Team Coaching: Facilitate team discussions to align on goals and develop collective strategies for adapting to change.

Example:

A leader uses the WISE model to help a team transition to a new project management software, addressing concerns and mapping out a successful implementation plan.

3. Agile Methodologies

Promoting Flexibility and Rapid Response

Definition: Agile methodologies, such as Scrum and Kanban, are iterative approaches to project management and software development that emphasize flexibility, collaboration, and customer feedback.

Key Principles:
- **Iterative Development:** Work is divided into small increments with frequent reassessment.
- **Collaboration:** Cross-functional teams work closely, often with daily communication.
- **Customer Focus:** Regular feedback from stakeholders guides adjustments.
- **Adaptability:** Plans are flexible to accommodate changes in requirements.

Benefits:
- **Enhanced Responsiveness:** Ability to adapt quickly to changes.
- **Improved Product Quality:** Continuous testing and feedback lead to better outcomes.
- **Increased Team Engagement:** Empowered teams take ownership of their work.

Case Study: Spotify's Agile Culture

Background: Spotify adopted a unique agile framework to support rapid innovation.

Outcome: The company scaled effectively while maintaining flexibility and a strong culture of collaboration.

Implementation Tips:

Training: Invest in agile training for leaders and teams.

Pilot Projects: Start with a small project to demonstrate value before scaling.

4. Change Management Frameworks

Structured Approaches to Organizational Transition

Definition: Change management frameworks provide structured methodologies for guiding organizations through transitions. The ADKAR model (Awareness, Desire, Knowledge, Ability, Reinforcement) is a widely used framework.

ADKAR Components:
- **Awareness:** Understanding the need for change.
- **Desire:** Supporting and participating in the change.
- **Knowledge:** Learning how to change.
- **Ability:** Implementing new skills and behaviors.
- **Reinforcement:** Sustaining the change.

Application:

- **Communication Plans:** Develop strategies to build awareness and desire.
- **Training Programs:** Provide knowledge and develop abilities.
- **Feedback Mechanisms:** Reinforce changes through recognition and support.

Case Study: Lewin's Change Management Model in Healthcare

Background: A hospital used Lewin's unfreeze-change-refreeze model to implement a new patient care system.

Outcome: Successful adoption of the system led to improved patient outcomes and staff satisfaction.

Tips for Leaders:

Engage Stakeholders Early: Involve employees in the planning process.

Monitor Progress: Use metrics to track adoption and address resistance.

5. Technology Adoption

Leveraging Digital Tools for Agility

Definition: Embracing technology enhances organizational agility by streamlining processes, improving communication, and enabling data-driven decision-making.

Key Technologies:

- **Collaboration Tools:** Platforms like Slack, Microsoft Teams, and Zoom facilitate communication among dispersed teams.
- **Cloud-Based Solutions:** Offer scalability and remote access to resources.
- **Data Analytics:** Tools that provide insights into market trends, customer behavior, and operational performance.

Benefits:

- **Efficiency Gains:** Automation reduces manual workload and errors.
- **Enhanced Decision-Making:** Real-time data supports strategic choices.
- **Competitive Advantage:** Early adoption can differentiate organizations.

Case Study: Digital Transformation at UPS

Background: UPS invested in advanced analytics and IoT to optimize delivery routes.

Outcome: Improved efficiency, reduced fuel consumption, and enhanced customer service.

Implementation Strategies:

Assess Needs: Identify areas where technology can have the most impact.

Invest in Training: Ensure employees are equipped to use new tools.

Adopt Incrementally: Phase in technology to manage costs and learning curves.

6. Lean Thinking

Maximizing Value by Minimizing Waste

Definition: Lean thinking focuses on delivering value to the customer by eliminating waste and optimizing processes.

Key Principles:

1. **Value Identification:** Define what provides value from the customer's perspective.

2. **Value Stream Mapping:** Analyze processes to identify waste.

3. **Flow Optimization:** Ensure smooth progression of products or services.

4. **Pull Systems:** Produce based on customer demand.

5. **Continuous Improvement (Kaizen):** Regularly seek ways to improve processes.

Application in Leadership:
- **Process Improvement Initiatives:** Lead efforts to streamline operations.
- **Employee Empowerment:** Involve team members in identifying inefficiencies.
- **Customer Focus:** Align activities with customer needs and expectations.

Case Study: Toyota Production System

Background: Toyota pioneered lean manufacturing, focusing on efficiency and quality.

Outcome: Achieved significant cost reductions and became a global industry leader.

Practical Exercise:

Value Stream Mapping Session: Map out a key process to identify and eliminate waste.

7. Crisis Communication Strategies

Effective Communication in Times of Uncertainty

Definition: Crisis communication involves planning and executing effective communication strategies during emergencies or significant disruptions.

Key Components:
- **Crisis Communication Plan:** Document outlining procedures, responsibilities, and protocols.
- **Key Messages:** Pre-defined messages that address stakeholder concerns.
- **Communication Channels:** Multiple platforms to disseminate information (e.g., email, social media, press releases).
- **Spokesperson Training:** Preparing designated individuals to communicate effectively.

Benefits:
- **Maintains Trust:** Transparent communication builds credibility.
- **Reduces Uncertainty:** Clear information alleviates confusion and rumors.
- **Guides Actions:** Provides stakeholders with instructions or next steps.

Case Study: Johnson & Johnson's Tylenol Crisis

Background: Faced with product tampering, Johnson & Johnson prioritized customer safety and transparent communication.

Outcome: Regained public trust and set a benchmark for crisis management.

Leadership Actions:
- **Timeliness:** Communicate promptly to stay ahead of misinformation.
- **Empathy:** Acknowledge the concerns and emotions of stakeholders.
- **Consistency:** Ensure all messages are aligned across channels.

8. Stakeholder Engagement

Building Trust Through Active Involvement

Definition: Stakeholder engagement involves actively involving those who are affected by or can influence organizational decisions, including employees, customers, suppliers, and regulators.

Key Practices:

- **Regular Communication:** Keep stakeholders informed about changes and developments.
- **Feedback Mechanisms:** Create channels for stakeholders to voice opinions and concerns.
- **Collaborative Decision-Making:** Involve stakeholders in planning and problem-solving.

Benefits:

- **Informed Decisions:** Diverse perspectives enhance decision quality.
- **Increased Buy-In:** Engagement fosters commitment to initiatives.
- **Risk Mitigation:** Early identification of potential issues through stakeholder input.

Case Study: Community Engagement in Urban Development

Background: A city council involved residents in planning a new park.

Outcome: The collaborative approach resulted in a space that met community needs and increased public support.

Implementation Tips:

Identify Key Stakeholders: Map out all relevant parties.

Tailor Engagement Methods: Use appropriate strategies for different stakeholder groups.

Follow-Up: Demonstrate how stakeholder input influenced outcomes.

9. Innovation Labs and Incubators

Nurturing Creativity and Experimentation

Definition: Innovation labs and incubators are dedicated spaces or programs within organizations designed to foster creativity, develop new ideas, and test innovative solutions.

Key Features:
- **Autonomy:** Teams have the freedom to explore without typical organizational constraints.
- **Resources:** Access to technology, funding, and expertise.
- **Collaboration:** Encourages cross-functional and cross-industry partnerships.

Benefits:
- **Accelerated Innovation:** Speeds up the development of new products or services.
- **Talent Attraction:** Appeals to creative professionals seeking dynamic environments.
- **Competitive Edge:** Positions organizations at the forefront of industry advancements.

Case Study: Google's X Lab

Background: Google's moonshot factory works on breakthrough technologies like self-driving cars and delivery drones.

Outcome: Generated innovations that have the potential to transform industries.

Steps to Establish an Innovation Lab:

1. **Define Objectives:** Clarify the lab's purpose and alignment with organizational goals.

2. **Select a Team:** Choose individuals with diverse skills and innovative mindsets.

3. **Provide Resources:** Allocate budget, technology, and workspace.

4. **Set Metrics:** Establish how success will be measured.

10. Adaptive Leadership Training

Developing Leaders for Dynamic Environments

Definition: Adaptive leadership training equips leaders with the skills and mindsets necessary to navigate complex challenges, embrace change, and inspire others to do the same.

Key Components:
- **Self-Awareness:** Understanding one's strengths, weaknesses, and impact on others.
- **Emotional Intelligence:** Managing emotions and relationships effectively.
- **Strategic Thinking:** Anticipating future trends and implications.

- **Decision-Making Under Uncertainty:** Making informed choices without complete information.

Benefits:
- **Enhanced Agility:** Leaders can pivot strategies as needed.
- **Employee Engagement:** Leaders inspire confidence and motivation.
- **Organizational Resilience:** Strong leadership fosters a culture that can withstand challenges.

Implementation Strategies:
- **Workshops and Seminars:** Offer training sessions focused on adaptive skills.
- **Coaching and Mentoring:** Provide personalized guidance from experienced leaders.
- **Experiential Learning:** Use simulations and real-world projects to apply concepts.

11. Cross-Functional Teams

Harnessing Diverse Expertise for Complex Challenges

Definition: Cross-functional teams consist of members from different departments or areas of expertise collaborating to achieve common goals.

Advantages:
- **Diverse Perspectives:** Combines varied knowledge and skills.
- **Innovation:** Sparks creativity through the intersection of ideas.
- **Improved Communication:** Breaks down silos within the organization.

Application in Adaptability:
- **Complex Problem-Solving:** Address multifaceted challenges more effectively.
- **Accelerated Learning:** Team members gain insights into other areas of the business.
- **Flexibility:** Teams can be reconfigured based on project needs.

Case Study: Apple's Product Development Teams

Background: Apple's success is partly attributed to its cross-functional teams integrating design, engineering, and marketing.

Outcome: Consistently delivers innovative products with cohesive user experiences.

Best Practices:
- **Clear Objectives:** Define team goals and individual roles.
- **Effective Leadership:** Appoint a leader skilled in managing diverse groups.
- **Open Communication:** Encourage transparency and regular updates.

12. Resilience Building Workshops

Strengthening the Capacity to Withstand and Grow from Adversity

Definition: Resilience building workshops focus on developing skills and strategies to cope with stress, adapt to change, and recover from setbacks.

Key Focus Areas:
- **Stress Management:** Techniques to handle pressure effectively.
- **Emotional Regulation:** Managing emotions in challenging situations.
- **Positive Mindset:** Cultivating optimism and hope.
- **Support Networks:** Building relationships that provide assistance and encouragement.

Benefits:
- **Enhanced Well-Being:** Supports mental and emotional health.
- **Increased Productivity:** Resilient individuals maintain performance under stress.
- **Organizational Health:** Contributes to a supportive and engaged workforce.

Implementation Tips:
- **Professional Facilitation:** Engage experts in psychology or organizational development.
- **Interactive Activities:** Use role-playing, discussions, and exercises.
- **Follow-Up Support:** Provide resources for ongoing development.

13. Crisis Simulation Exercises

Preparing for the Unexpected Through Practice

Definition: Crisis simulation exercises are mock scenarios that test an organization's readiness to handle emergencies and unexpected events.

Objectives:
- **Identify Gaps:** Reveal weaknesses in plans and procedures.
- **Enhance Coordination:** Improve communication and teamwork under pressure.
- **Build Confidence:** Familiarity with crisis protocols reduces anxiety.

Types of Simulations:
- **Tabletop Exercises:** Discussion-based sessions reviewing responses to hypothetical situations.
- **Functional Exercises:** Simulate specific functions (e.g., communication systems) without full deployment.
- **Full-Scale Exercises:** Realistic enactments involving multiple stakeholders.

Case Study: Financial Institutions' Stress Testing

Background: Banks conduct simulations to assess responses to economic downturns.

Outcome: Improved risk management and compliance with regulatory requirements.

Implementation Steps:
- **Define Objectives:** Clarify what the exercise aims to achieve.
- **Design Scenarios:** Develop realistic and challenging situations.
- **Assign Roles:** Ensure participants understand their responsibilities.
- **Debrief:** Analyze performance and identify improvement areas.

14. Key Performance Indicators (KPIs) for Adaptability

Measuring and Monitoring Adaptation Efforts

Definition: KPIs for adaptability are metrics that help organizations track their ability to respond to change effectively.

Examples of Adaptability KPIs:
- **Time to Market:** Speed of launching new products or services.
- **Employee Turnover Rate:** Indicator of employee satisfaction and adaptability.
- **Innovation Rate:** Percentage of revenue from new products or services.
- **Customer Satisfaction Scores:** Reflects responsiveness to customer needs.
- **Training Hours:** Investment in employee development.

Benefits:
- **Informed Decision-Making:** Data-driven insights guide strategic adjustments.
- **Accountability:** Establishes expectations for performance.
- **Continuous Improvement:** Identifies trends and areas for enhancement.

Implementation Tips:
- **Align with Goals:** KPIs should support organizational objectives.
- **Regular Reporting:** Monitor metrics consistently.

- **Adjust as Needed:** Update KPIs to remain relevant in changing environments.

15. Customer Feedback Loops

Leveraging Customer Insights for Continuous Improvement

Definition: Customer feedback loops are processes for collecting, analyzing, and acting on customer input to enhance products, services, and experiences.

Methods:

- **Surveys and Questionnaires:** Gather quantitative and qualitative data.
- **Focus Groups:** In-depth discussions with selected customers.
- **Social Media Monitoring:** Track mentions and sentiments online.
- **Customer Interviews:** Direct conversations to understand needs and preferences.

Benefits:

- **Customer-Centric Improvements:** Align offerings with customer expectations.
- **Increased Loyalty:** Demonstrates commitment to customer satisfaction.
- **Early Issue Detection:** Identify problems before they escalate.

Case Study: Starbucks' Customer Engagement

Background: Starbucks uses its My Starbucks Idea platform to solicit suggestions.

Outcome: Implemented numerous customer-generated ideas, enhancing loyalty and innovation.

Best Practices:
- **Act on Feedback:** Show customers that their input leads to tangible changes.
- **Close the Loop:** Inform customers about actions taken in response to their feedback.
- **Integrate Across Departments:** Ensure insights inform all relevant areas of the business.

16. Networking and Industry Benchmarking

Learning from Peers and Industry Leaders

Definition: Networking and benchmarking involve comparing organizational practices and performance metrics with peers to identify best practices and areas for improvement.

Activities:
- **Industry Conferences:** Attend events to learn about trends and innovations.
- **Professional Associations:** Join groups relevant to your field.
- **Benchmarking Studies:** Participate in surveys and reports that analyze industry data.
- **Peer Collaborations:** Engage in knowledge-sharing with other organizations.

Benefits:
- **Stay Informed:** Keep up-to-date with industry developments.
- **Identify Gaps:** Understand where your organization stands relative to others.
- **Inspiration:** Discover new ideas and strategies.

Implementation Tips:
- **Set Objectives:** Define what you aim to achieve through networking.
- **Be Proactive:** Reach out to peers and participate actively.
- **Share Wisely:** Balance sharing insights with maintaining competitive advantages.

17. Resource Allocation Models

Flexibility in Deploying Resources

Definition: Flexible resource allocation models allow organizations to redistribute resources quickly based on changing priorities and emerging opportunities.

Key Concepts:
- **Dynamic Budgeting:** Adjust budgets in response to real-time data and market conditions.
- **Project-Based Allocation:** Assign resources to projects rather than departments.
- **Portfolio Management:** Evaluate and prioritize initiatives based on strategic value.

Benefits:
- **Agility:** Respond swiftly to new opportunities or challenges.

- **Efficiency:** Optimize the use of resources for maximum impact.
- **Strategic Alignment:** Ensure investments support organizational goals.

Implementation Strategies:

- **Regular Reviews:** Schedule frequent assessments of resource allocation.
- **Transparent Criteria:** Establish clear guidelines for decision-making.
- **Empower Managers:** Allow those closest to the work to make allocation decisions within parameters.

18. Futurist Thinking

Anticipating Long-Term Trends and Disruptions

Definition: Futurist thinking involves exploring and predicting future trends, technologies, and societal shifts to inform strategic planning.

Approaches:

- **Environmental Scanning:** Monitor global developments across various domains.
- **Trend Analysis:** Identify patterns that indicate emerging changes.
- **Expert Consultations:** Engage with thought leaders and futurists.
- **Scenario Development:** Envision long-term possibilities beyond traditional planning horizons.

Benefits:

- **Proactive Strategy Development:** Prepare for potential disruptions before they occur.
- **Innovation Opportunities:** Identify areas for early investment.
- **Risk Mitigation:** Anticipate challenges and develop contingency plans.

Implementation Tips:

- **Allocate Time for Exploration:** Encourage leaders to dedicate time to futurist activities.
- **Cross-Disciplinary Learning:** Draw insights from various fields.
- **Incorporate into Planning:** Use futurist insights to inform strategic decisions.

19. Cultivating an Adaptive Culture

Embedding Adaptability into Organizational DNA

Definition: An adaptive culture prioritizes learning, flexibility, and responsiveness at all organizational levels.

Key Elements:

- **Shared Values:** Embrace change as a core value.
- **Learning Orientation:** Encourage continuous development and knowledge sharing.
- **Empowerment:** Allow employees to make decisions and take initiative.
- **Feedback Culture:** Promote open communication and constructive criticism.

Benefits:
- **Resilience:** Organizations can withstand and thrive amidst change.
- **Employee Engagement:** A dynamic culture attracts and retains talent.
- **Innovation:** An adaptive culture fosters creativity and experimentation.

Strategies for Leaders:
- **Model Adaptability:** Demonstrate flexibility and openness to change.
- **Recognize Adaptable Behaviors:** Celebrate individuals and teams that exemplify adaptability.
- **Align Systems and Processes:** Ensure policies and procedures support, rather than hinder, adaptability.

20. Strategic Alliances and Partnerships

Collaborative Approaches to Expansion and Innovation

Definition: Strategic alliances and partnerships involve collaborating with other organizations to achieve mutual goals, leveraging combined resources and expertise.

Types of Partnerships:
- **Joint Ventures:** Create a new entity owned by partnering organizations.
- **Licensing Agreements:** Share technology or products.
- **Supply Chain Partnerships:** Collaborate with suppliers for mutual benefits.
- **Research Collaborations:** Work together on innovation and development.

Benefits:
- **Resource Sharing:** Access to additional capital, technology, or skills.
- **Market Expansion:** Enter new markets or customer segments.
- **Risk Sharing:** Distribute the risks associated with new ventures.

Case Study: Starbucks and Barnes & Noble

Background: Starbucks partnered with Barnes & Noble to place coffee shops within bookstores.

Outcome: Enhanced customer experience and increased foot traffic for both companies.

Implementation Tips:
- **Align Objectives:** Ensure both parties have compatible goals.
- **Establish Clear Agreements:** Define roles, responsibilities, and expectations.
- **Maintain Open Communication:** Regularly discuss progress and address issues.

Integrating the Holistic Intelligence Model

Applying these tools and techniques aligns with the Holistic Intelligence Model by enhancing various intelligences:

1. **Analytical Intelligence (AQ):** Utilizing data analytics, KPIs, and trend analysis sharpens critical thinking and decision-making.

2. **Creative Intelligence (CrQ):** Innovation labs, agile methodologies, and futurist thinking foster creativity and innovation.

3. **Practical Intelligence (PQ):** Implementing change management frameworks and lean thinking translates knowledge into effective action.

4. **Emotional Resilience (ER):** Resilience workshops and adaptive leadership training build capacity to handle stress and adapt emotionally.

5. **Interpersonal Intelligence:** Stakeholder engagement and cross-functional teams enhance communication and collaboration skills.

6. **Cultural Intelligence (CQ):** Networking, industry benchmarking, and strategic alliances promote understanding across cultures and industries.

7. **Intrapersonal Intelligence:** Reflecting on experiences through exercises and training enhances self-awareness.

8. **Ethical Intelligence (EthQ):** Ethical considerations in technology adoption and change initiatives ensure integrity and social responsibility.

—

Effectively adapting to change and uncertainty requires a multifaceted approach. By leveraging a diverse set of tools and techniques, leaders can enhance their own adaptability and foster resilient, innovative organizations. Embracing change as an opportunity, cultivating an adaptive culture, and continuously developing skills and strategies will position leaders and their teams to navigate the complexities of the modern business environment successfully.

Remember, adaptability is a journey of continuous learning and growth. By integrating these tools and techniques into your leadership practice, you not only enhance your ability to navigate change but also inspire those around you to embrace uncertainty as a pathway to innovation and success.

Introducing GROW Analysis: A Comprehensive Framework for Strategic Development

William Stanek's GROW analysis—standing for Gains, Realities, Opportunities, Weaknesses—is a strategic tool designed to provide a holistic understanding of an organization's or individual's current state. It serves as an alternative to the traditional SWOT analysis, offering a more nuanced approach by emphasizing internal gains and the realities of both internal and external environments. By leveraging GROW analysis, leaders and organizations can make informed decisions, set realistic goals, and navigate their strategic journeys with purpose and resilience.

Components of GROW Analysis

1. Gains (Internal Factors)

Description: Gains represent the internal strengths, advantages, and positive attributes that an organization or individual possesses. These are the assets that contribute to success and provide a competitive edge.

Examples:
- **Accomplishments and Achievements:** Recognizing and celebrating milestones boosts confidence and motivation.
- **Specialized Skills and Expertise:** Unique knowledge or expertise in a particular field.

- **Strong Professional Network:** Established relationships with colleagues, mentors, or industry peers.
- **Resilience and Adaptability:** The ability to recover from challenges and adjust to new situations.
- **Positive Mindset and Attitude:** Maintaining optimism leads to increased productivity and creativity.
- **High Emotional Intelligence:** Effective interpersonal skills enhance relationships and leadership abilities.
- **Resourcefulness and Creativity:** Innovative problem-solving capabilities.

2. Realities (Internal and External Factors)

Description: Realities refer to the current state or situation, encompassing an honest assessment of both internal conditions and external environments. Recognizing realities is crucial for setting realistic goals and making informed decisions.

Examples:
- **Resource Limitations:** Constraints such as budget, time, or manpower.
- **Skill Gaps:** Areas where additional training or development is needed.
- **Current Workload and Commitments:** Existing responsibilities that affect capacity.
- **Past Failures or Setbacks:** Lessons learned from previous challenges.
- **Feedback and Evaluation Results:** Insights from peers, supervisors, or performance evaluations.
- **Market Trends and Competitor Analysis:** Understanding industry dynamics.

- **Personal Health and Well-being:** Physical and mental health considerations.

3. Opportunities (External Factors)

Description: Opportunities are external circumstances that can be leveraged for positive outcomes. They represent potential areas for growth, development, or improvement.

Examples:
- **Emerging Technologies and Trends:** Adopting new technologies can lead to innovation.
- **Market Demand and Niche Identification:** Identifying unmet needs in the market.
- **Networking and Collaboration:** Building strategic partnerships.
- **Changing Consumer Preferences:** Adapting to evolving customer needs.
- **Legislation and Regulatory Changes:** Complying with new regulations can offer advantages.
- **Global Expansion:** Exploring international markets.
- **Mergers and Strategic Alliances:** Synergistic growth opportunities.

4. Weaknesses (Internal Factors)

Description: Weaknesses are internal limitations or areas needing improvement. Acknowledging weaknesses is essential for growth and mitigating potential hindrances.

Examples:
- **Skill Gaps or Lack of Expertise:** Identifying areas for development.

- **Inefficiencies or Bottlenecks:** Operational challenges that need addressing.
- **Communication Issues:** Barriers to effective collaboration.
- **Inadequate Resources:** Managing with limited resources or budget constraints.
- **Lack of Clear Goals:** The need for defined objectives and priorities.
- **Resistance to Change:** Overcoming reluctance to adopt new strategies.
- **Lack of Diversity or Inclusion:** Fostering an inclusive culture for innovation.

Implementing GROW Analysis

1. Conducting a Comprehensive Assessment

- **Internal Evaluation:** Identify and list all internal gains and weaknesses.
- **External Evaluation:** Examine external realities and opportunities.
- **Honest Reflection:** Encourage transparency to ensure an accurate analysis.

2. Strategic Planning

- **Leverage Gains:** Utilize strengths to capitalize on opportunities.
- **Address Weaknesses:** Develop plans to improve or mitigate internal limitations.
- **Acknowledge Realities:** Set realistic goals based on current conditions.
- **Seize Opportunities:** Proactively pursue external prospects for growth.

3. Action Plan Development

- **Set Clear Objectives:** Define what success looks like.
- **Allocate Resources:** Determine what is needed to achieve goals.
- **Assign Responsibilities:** Clarify who is accountable for each action.
- **Establish Timelines:** Set deadlines for achieving milestones.

4. Continuous Monitoring and Adaptation

- **Regular Reviews:** Schedule periodic assessments to track progress.
- **Adjust Strategies:** Be prepared to modify plans based on new insights or changes.
- **Celebrate Achievements:** Recognize progress to maintain motivation.

Benefits of GROW Analysis

- **Holistic Perspective:** Provides a comprehensive view by combining internal and external factors.
- **Enhanced Decision-Making:** Informs strategic choices with a balanced understanding of strengths and limitations.
- **Goal Alignment:** Ensures objectives are realistic and aligned with actual capabilities and market conditions.
- **Proactive Approach:** Encourages anticipation of challenges and identification of opportunities.
- **Personal and Professional Development:** Fosters self-awareness and continuous improvement.

GROW Analysis vs. SWOT Analysis

While both GROW and SWOT analyses are strategic tools used for evaluation, they differ in focus and approach:

GROW Analysis:

- **Gains** instead of **Strengths**: Emphasizes positive internal factors and achievements.
- **Realities** encompass both internal and external factors, providing a nuanced understanding of the current state.
- **Opportunities** remain as external possibilities for advancement.
- **Weaknesses** are internal areas needing improvement.
- **Focuses on Growth and Development:** Encourages ongoing evaluation and adaptability.

SWOT Analysis:

- **Strengths and Weaknesses:** Internal factors.
- **Opportunities and Threats:** External factors.
- **Threats** are potential external challenges or obstacles.
- **Static Snapshot:** Often provides a one-time assessment without emphasizing continuous adaptation.

Integrating GROW Analysis into Leadership Practices

1. Empower Informed Decision-Making

Leaders can make strategic choices grounded in a comprehensive understanding of their organization's or team's capabilities and the external environment.

2. Enhance Strategic Planning

By acknowledging realities and leveraging gains, leaders can set achievable goals and develop effective strategies.

3. Foster a Growth Mindset

Encourages a culture of continuous improvement, adaptability, and resilience.

4. Improve Communication

Sharing the GROW analysis with team members promotes transparency and collective ownership of objectives and challenges.

5. Drive Innovation

Identifying opportunities and addressing weaknesses can lead to innovative solutions and competitive advantages.

The GROW Analysis serves as a dynamic and comprehensive framework for strategic planning and development. By focusing on **Gains**, acknowledging **Realities**, identifying **Opportunities**, and addressing **Weaknesses**, individuals and organizations can create actionable strategies that are both realistic and aspirational.

Incorporating GROW analysis empowers leaders to:

- Navigate complex environments with confidence.
- Allocate resources effectively.
- Adapt to changing circumstances with agility.
- Cultivate resilience and a proactive mindset.
- Achieve sustained personal and professional growth.

Ready to Implement GROW Analysis?

- **Start with Self-Assessment:** Reflect on your personal or organizational gains and weaknesses.
- **Acknowledge Your Realities:** Be honest about your current situation and external factors.
- **Identify Opportunities:** Look for external trends or gaps you can capitalize on.
- **Develop an Action Plan:** Leverage your gains, address weaknesses, and pursue opportunities.
- **Monitor Progress:** Regularly revisit your GROW analysis to stay aligned and make necessary adjustments.

By embracing the GROW framework, you equip yourself with a powerful tool to guide your strategic journey toward success and fulfillment.

Deep Dive: GROW Analysis

Conduct a comprehensive GROW analysis to assess the internal and external factors affecting the organization. This analysis provides valuable insights for strategic decision-making.

These examples illustrate how the GROW analysis methodically evaluates gains, realities, opportunities, and weaknesses in various real-world scenarios, aiding in strategic decision-making amidst change and uncertainty.

Real-World Scenarios Using GROW Analysis

Business Expansion Strategy

Goal:

- To expand the company's market presence into new international markets within the next two years, increasing revenue by 30%.

Gains:

- **Accomplishments:** The company has a robust portfolio and established brand reputation in the domestic market.
- **Specialized Skills:** In-depth knowledge of local consumer behavior and preferences.
- **Strong Professional Network:** Partnerships with distributors and suppliers abroad.

Realities:

- **Resource Limitations:** Limited initial investment for international expansion.
- **Skill Gaps:** Lack of experience in navigating international regulatory frameworks.
- **Market Trends:** Increasing demand for the company's products in target international markets.

Opportunities:

- **Emerging Markets:** Identified emerging markets with similar consumer demographics.
- **Networking and Collaboration:** Potential collaborations with local distributors and industry partners abroad.
- **Global Expansion:** Growing interest among consumers for international brands.

Weaknesses:

- **Inadequate Resources:** Limited capital and human resources for managing global expansion.
- **Lack of Expertise:** Lack of familiarity with international trade laws and market dynamics.
- **Communication Challenges:** Potential language barriers and cultural differences.

Educational Institution's Learning Initiative

Goal:

- To implement a personalized learning program for students, improving overall academic performance by 20% within a year.

Gains:

- **Accomplishments:** Previous successful implementation of technology-based learning modules.
- **Specialized Skills:** Proficient in developing adaptive learning systems.
- **High Emotional Intelligence:** Teachers and staff with strong empathy and student-centric approach.

Realities:

- **Skill Gaps:** Lack of comprehensive data analytics for individual student performance tracking.
- **Feedback and Evaluation:** Positive response from students and parents on innovative learning methodologies.
- **Past Failures:** Previous unsuccessful attempts at personalized learning initiatives due to technology limitations.

Opportunities:
- **Emerging Technologies:** Availability of advanced learning management systems for personalized education.
- **Feedback and Evaluation:** Positive feedback from pilot programs on personalized learning.
- **Changing Education Policies:** Supportive policies promoting innovative teaching methodologies.

Weaknesses:
- **Resource Constraints:** Limited budget for acquiring advanced learning tools.
- **Inadequate Data:** Lack of comprehensive student performance data for individualized learning.
- b Teacher apprehension regarding adopting new teaching methods.

Nonprofit Organization's Fundraising Strategy

Goal:
- To raise funds and secure partnerships to support a community development project, increasing outreach by 40% within six months.

Gains:
- **Strong Professional Network:** Existing relationships with local businesses and community leaders.
- **Resourcefulness:** Experience in organizing successful local fundraising events.
- **Resilience and Adaptability:** Previous successes in adapting to changing donor preferences.

Realities:

- **Resource Limitations:** Limited funds and resources for large-scale projects.
- **Past Failures:** Previous unsuccessful attempts at securing government grants for similar projects.
- **Market Trends:** Growing interest among local businesses in supporting community initiatives.

Opportunities:

- **Networking and Collaboration:** Potential collaborations with larger NGOs or corporations for funding.
- **Changing Donor Preferences:** Increasing interest among younger donors in community-centric projects.
- **Market Expansion:** Potential partnerships with local businesses for sponsorship opportunities.

Weaknesses:

- **Lack of Clear Strategy:** No defined long-term fundraising strategy.
- **Resistance to Change:** Apathy or skepticism from some community stakeholders toward new projects.
- **Limited Expertise:** Lack of experienced grant writers or fundraising experts in the organization.

Fostering Adaptability in Your Team

- "Embracing adaptability is embracing the future; as leaders commit to this principle, they unlock the potential to lead with resilience and innovation."

As a leader, your ability to cultivate adaptability within your team is as crucial as developing it within yourself. An adaptable team is resilient, innovative, and better equipped to handle the challenges of a dynamic environment. This section explores strategies to promote adaptability among team members, leveraging the Holistic Intelligence Model and practical techniques to empower your team to thrive amidst change.

The Role of Leaders in Cultivating Team Adaptability

Modeling Adaptable Behaviors
- **Lead by Example:** Demonstrate flexibility and openness to change in your actions.
- **Share Experiences:** Discuss your own challenges and how you adapted.
- **Display Emotional Resilience:** Show composure under pressure, setting a tone for the team.

Creating a Supportive Environment
- **Psychological Safety:** Foster an atmosphere where team members feel safe to express ideas and concerns.

- **Open Communication:** Encourage transparency and dialogue.
- **Recognition:** Acknowledge and reward adaptability and innovation.

Empowering Team Members

- **Delegate Authority:** Give team members autonomy to make decisions.
- **Provide Resources:** Offer tools and training to develop adaptability skills.
- **Encourage Risk-Taking:** Support experimentation and learning from failures.

Strategies to Promote Adaptability

1. Encourage Continuous Learning

Actions:

- **Professional Development:** Provide access to training programs and workshops.
- **Learning Culture:** Promote knowledge sharing through team meetings or internal forums.
- **Personal Development Plans:** Collaborate with team members to set learning goals.

Benefits:

- **Skill Enhancement:** Keeps skills current and relevant.
- Employee Engagement: Increases motivation and job satisfaction.
- **Organizational Agility:** Builds a workforce capable of adapting to new demands.

2. Promote a Growth Mindset

Actions:

- **Challenge Fixed Beliefs:** Encourage team members to view abilities as developable.
- **Set Stretch Goals:** Assign tasks that push boundaries and require new approaches.
- **Provide Constructive Feedback:** Focus on effort and learning rather than just outcomes.

Benefits:

- **Increased Resilience:** Team members are more likely to persevere through challenges.
- **Enhanced Innovation:** Openness to new ideas leads to creative solutions.
- **Improved Performance:** Continuous improvement becomes a norm.

3. Provide Challenging Assignments

Actions:

- **Rotate Roles:** Offer opportunities to work in different functions or projects.
- **Assign Complex Problems:** Engage team members in solving multifaceted issues.
- **Encourage Cross-Training:** Facilitate learning across different areas of expertise.

Benefits:

- **Skill Diversification:** Expands capabilities and adaptability.
- **Team Cohesion:** Strengthens collaboration and understanding among team members.

- **Preparedness:** Builds readiness for future challenges.

4. Encourage Innovation and Creativity

Actions:

- **Idea Generation Sessions:** Host brainstorming meetings.
- **Innovation Challenges:** Create competitions to solve organizational problems.
- **Resource Allocation:** Dedicate time and budget for experimental projects.

Benefits:

- **Enhanced Problem-Solving:** Diverse ideas lead to better solutions.
- **Employee Empowerment:** Increases ownership and engagement.
- **Competitive Advantage:** Drives differentiation in the market.

5. Provide Support During Change

Actions:

- **Clear Communication:** Keep the team informed about changes and the reasons behind them.
- **Offer Training:** Provide resources to develop necessary skills for new initiatives.
- **Emotional Support:** Be available to discuss concerns and provide reassurance.

Benefits:

- **Smooth Transitions:** Reduces resistance and confusion.

- **Maintained Morale:** Supports team well-being and productivity.
- **Trust Building:** Strengthens relationships within the team.

Integrating the Holistic Intelligence Model

Applying the 8 Pillars of the Holistic Intelligence Model to foster adaptability in your team:

1. Emotional Resilience (ER):

- **Team Activities:** Organize workshops on stress management.
- **Support Systems:** Encourage peer support networks within the team.

2. Creative Intelligence (CrQ):

- **Innovation Labs:** Establish spaces for creative exploration.
- **Design Thinking:** Train the team in methodologies that promote creative problem-solving.

3. Practical Intelligence (PQ):

- **Real-World Projects:** Assign tasks that require practical application of skills.
- **Mentorship Programs:** Pair less experienced team members with seasoned professionals.

4. Cultural Intelligence (CQ):

- **Diversity Initiatives:** Promote inclusive practices and celebrate different perspectives.
- **Global Collaboration:** Facilitate interactions with international teams or clients.

5. Intrapersonal Intelligence:
- **Self-Reflection Exercises:** Encourage journaling or mindfulness practices.
- **Personal Development Workshops:** Offer sessions on self-awareness and emotional intelligence.

6. Interpersonal Intelligence:
- **Team-Building Activities:** Conduct events that strengthen relationships.
- **Communication Training:** Provide resources to enhance interpersonal skills.

7. Ethical Intelligence (EthQ):
- **Ethics Training:** Discuss ethical considerations in decision-making.
- **Values Alignment:** Ensure team goals align with organizational values.

8. Analytical Intelligence (AQ):
- **Data Literacy Programs:** Improve the team's ability to interpret and use data.
- **Critical Thinking Exercises:** Engage in activities that enhance analytical skills.

Practical Exercises for Developing Team Adaptability

Exercise 1: Adaptability Workshops

Purpose: Provide structured learning experiences focused on developing adaptability skills.

Components:

Interactive Sessions: Include role-playing, simulations, and group discussions.

Expert Facilitators: Engage professionals with expertise in adaptability and change management.

Action Plans: Have participants develop personal strategies for enhancing adaptability.

Exercise 2: Team Reflection Meetings

Purpose: Create space for collective reflection on experiences and learnings.

Process:

Schedule Regular Meetings: Set aside time after significant projects or changes.

Facilitate Open Dialogue: Encourage honest sharing of successes and challenges.

Document Insights: Capture key takeaways and action items.

Exercise 3: Innovation Hackathons

Purpose: Stimulate creativity and collaborative problem-solving.

Structure:

Define Challenges: Identify organizational issues or opportunities.

Form Diverse Teams: Mix different roles and skill sets.

Set Timeframes: Create a sense of urgency with time-bound events.

Present Solutions: Have teams share their ideas with leadership.

Exercise 4: Mentorship Circles

Purpose: Foster knowledge sharing and support networks.

Implementation:

Group Mentoring: Organize small groups with a mentor to discuss adaptability topics.

Peer Learning: Encourage mutual learning among team members.

Goal Setting: Assist participants in setting and achieving adaptability goals.

Reflection Questions

1. Assessing Team Dynamics:
- How adaptable is your team currently?
- What factors are influencing your team's ability to adapt?

2. Leadership Influence:
- In what ways are you modeling adaptability for your team?
- How do your actions encourage or hinder adaptability?

3. Support Mechanisms:
- What resources are available to your team to develop adaptability?
- How can you enhance support for learning and growth?

4. Cultural Considerations:
- Does your organizational culture promote or resist change?
- What steps can you take to align culture with adaptability goals?

5. Future Planning:
- What upcoming changes might impact your team?
- How can you prepare your team to navigate these changes successfully?

Case Study: Fostering Adaptability at Adobe

Background:

Challenge: Adobe decided to shift from selling boxed software to a cloud-based subscription model.

Impact on Teams: Required significant changes in development processes, sales strategies, and customer engagement.

Leadership Actions:

Transparent Communication: Leaders openly discussed the reasons and benefits of the change.

Training Programs: Provided extensive training to equip employees with new skills.

Innovation Encouragement: Empowered teams to experiment with new ideas and approaches.

Recognition: Celebrated successes and acknowledged efforts during the transition.

Outcomes:

Successful Transformation: Adobe smoothly transitioned to a subscription model, increasing revenue and customer satisfaction.

Employee Engagement: Maintained high levels of engagement and reduced turnover during the change.

Enhanced Innovation: The culture of adaptability led to continued innovation in products and services.

Lessons Learned:

Leadership Commitment: Strong leadership is crucial in guiding teams through change.

Empowering Teams: Providing support and autonomy enables teams to adapt effectively.

Continuous Communication: Keeping teams informed reduces uncertainty and builds trust.

Fostering adaptability in your team is a multifaceted endeavor that requires intentional actions and a supportive environment. By modeling adaptable behaviors, creating opportunities for growth, and leveraging the Holistic Intelligence Model, leaders can cultivate teams that not only cope with change but excel in dynamic environments.

An adaptable team is a resilient team—one that can navigate the uncertainties of today's world with confidence and creativity. As a leader, your commitment to developing this competency within your team will not only enhance performance but also position your organization for sustained success in the face of change.

Adaptability is more than a skill; it's a mindset and a cultural attribute that, when embraced, transforms organizations. As you continue on your leadership journey, remember that your ability to adapt and to foster adaptability in others is a cornerstone of effective leadership in the modern era. Embrace change as an ally, encourage continuous learning, and lead with the confidence that you and your team can navigate whatever the future holds.

Inspirational Quotes

- **Charles Darwin:** "It is not the strongest of the species that survives, nor the most intelligent, but the one most responsive to change."

- **Jack Welch:** "Change before you have to."
- **Rosabeth Moss Kanter:** "The happiest people are the ones who have a vision for where they are going, and they're flexible enough to find new routes to get there."

Thoughtful Exploration: Thriving in Amidst Flux for Leaders

These thought-provoking questions are crafted to stimulate contemplative discussion and reflection on the challenges and opportunities presented in this book. They prompt readers to consider practical strategies for thriving in dynamic and unpredictable environments.

- How do you define adaptability within a leadership context, and why is it paramount for leaders to flourish in dynamic environments?

- Can you recall a specific instance where a leader adeptly navigated a major change or uncertainty? What strategies did they employ that contributed to their success?

- What are some prevalent challenges that leaders may encounter when grappling with change and uncertainty? How can they proactively address these challenges?

- In what ways does an organization's culture influence its ability to adapt to change and uncertainty? What role does leadership play in shaping and sustaining a culture of adaptability?

- In your view, what are the key skills or traits that leaders need to cultivate in order to excel in dynamic environments? How can these be developed and fortified?

- Can you think of an example where a leader struggled to adapt to a significant change? What were the repercussions of their inability to thrive in that dynamic situation?

- How do you personally approach and handle change and uncertainty? Are there any strategies from this book that you would like to integrate into your own leadership style?

- What are some potential benefits that can arise from successfully navigating change and uncertainty as a leader? How can these benefits contribute to the overall success of an organization?

- These questions can serve as discussion prompts to foster contemplative reflection and meaningful conversations about the concepts covered in the book. They can be tailored to suit various learning environments and objectives, making them a versatile resource for diverse audiences.

For Book Discussion Groups, Reading Discussion Groups, and classrooms dedicated to leadership development, these prompts provide invaluable resources. They provide a structured framework for engaging and enriching discussions about the content, enabling participants to share their insights and perspectives.

Additional Suggestions:

- Encourage participants to draw from personal experiences or real-world examples when responding to the prompts.

- Cultivate a safe and inclusive environment for sharing thoughts and opinions.

- Consider assigning specific questions to different individuals or groups to ensure a well-rounded discussion.
- Customize the questions to align with the specific context and learning goals of your group.

Remember, the aim of these discussion prompts is to deepen understanding, foster critical thinking, and facilitate meaningful exchanges among participants. Feel free to adapt them to best serve your unique learning or teaching environment.

Enjoy your discussions!

About the Author:
William R. Stanek

Meet the Visionary, the Storyteller, and Your Guide on the Journey to Intentional Living

Biography

William R. Stanek is no ordinary author in the world of personal growth. With a background that's woven with more experiences than can be counted, Stanek is known for his straightforward wisdom, practical insights, and a talent for helping others build lives that align with their core values. His work speaks to those who seek authenticity and a real connection to their purpose, bringing an inspiring yet realistic approach to the journey of self-discovery.

Throughout his journey, Stanek has played many roles—teacher, innovator, mentor, and artist—each experience adding to the perspective he shares in his books. He is known for being the voice people turn to when conventional advice falls short and when what's needed isn't a quick fix but a path to meaningful change. Over his career, he has helped countless individuals rethink their relationship with success, personal growth, and what it truly means to live a purposeful life.

As a leader and technologist at the intersection of business, technology, and leadership, William's work extends far beyond the written word. He has spent years inspiring action, driving meaningful change, and guiding others on how to create impact that resonates, endures, and honors each individual's unique journey. His influence spans professions and walks of life, providing a grounding perspective in a world that often encourages us to chase everything at once. In this book, William shares his experiences, insights, and deep conviction in the power of intentional living with a broader audience.

Connect with William R. Stanek

Join William in exploring new ideas, challenging conventional wisdom, and pushing the boundaries of what's possible in personal growth. Connect with him here:

LinkedIn: Follow William for updates, articles, and perspectives on intentional living and personal growth.

https://www.linkedin.com/in/williamstanek/

Facebook: Like his author page for daily insights, reflections, and updates.

http://www.facebook.com/William.Stanek.Author

Twitter: Follow for thought-provoking tweets and personal growth tips in 280 characters.

http://www.twitter.com/WilliamStanek

Website: Visit http://www.williamrstanek.com to learn more about his books, workshops, and other projects.

Comprehensive Professional and Collegiate Reference Edition

William R. Stanek

Esteemed author, renowned worldwide bestseller, and trusted consultant to Fortune 100, 500, and 1000 companies for over three decades.

THE RESILIENT LEADER
EMBRACING RESILIENCE FOR SUCCESS

REIMAGINING LEADERSHIP BEYOND THE EQ VS IQ PARADIGM

Actionable Leadership Principles - Straightforward and Effective

The "Comprehensive Professional and Collegiate Reference Edition" offers enhanced value through additional comprehension aids, including comprehensive insights, holistic analysis, discussion prompts, independent study notes, and teacher/facilitator guidance.

THE NEW LEADERSHIP LANDSCAPE

WILLIAM'S EXPERTISE IS THE BEST-KEPT SECRET AMONG TOP MANAGEMENT, DELIVERING UNPARALLELED IMPACT.

"The Resilient Leader, Embracing Resilience for Success" stands out in the crowded landscape of leadership and emotional intelligence books by offering a fresh, holistic approach to leadership that transcends traditional models. This groundbreaking work by William R. Stanek redefines the essence of effective leadership in the modern era, distinguishing itself through several key differentiators:

- **Holistic Integration of Multiple Intelligences**   While most leadership books focus on emotional intelligence (EQ) or traditional cognitive intelligence (IQ), "The Resilient Leader, Embracing Resilience for Success" introduces readers to the 8 Pillars of Leadership. This innovative framework encompasses Emotional Resilience, Creative Intelligence, Practical Intelligence, Cultural Intelligence, Intrapersonal Intelligence, Interpersonal Intelligence, Ethical Intelligence, and Analytical Intelligence. By embracing a broader spectrum of intelligences, the book equips leaders with a multifaceted toolkit, enabling them to navigate the complexities of the contemporary landscape more effectively than ever before.

- **Emphasis on Emotional Resilience**   "The Resilient Leader, Embracing Resilience for Success" delves deep into emotional resilience, offering readers actionable strategies to cultivate this essential trait. The book presents emotional resilience as the bedrock of leadership excellence, enabling leaders to withstand challenges, adapt to change, thrive in adversity, and so much more. Whereas most literature on emotional intelligence or emotional resilience treats resilience as a narrow set of traits or a subset of emotional intelligence, "The Resilient Leader, Embracing Resilience for Success" reconceptualizes it as a multifaceted intelligence in its own right. This book goes far beyond the typical definitions and presents emotional resilience as a complex, dynamic intelligence that is critical for effective leadership.

- **Rigorous Self-Assessment Tool**   Distinct from other leadership books that offer generalized advice, "The

Resilient Leader, Embracing Resilience for Success" integrates a cutting-edge self-assessment tool. This personalized assessment allows readers to evaluate their strengths and areas for growth, providing a tailored roadmap for personal and professional development. This actionable, data-driven approach ensures that readers can make concrete progress on their leadership journey.

- **Case Studies and Real-World Application** While many books on leadership and emotional intelligence rely on theoretical principles, "The Resilient Leader, Embracing Resilience for Success" grounds its insights in practical reality. Through a series of detailed case studies featuring real-world scenarios and leadership challenges, the book illustrates how the principles of resilient leadership can be applied in various contexts. From crisis management in the financial sector to navigating complex mergers and leading through global pandemics, these case studies offer readers a window into the transformative power of resilient leadership in action.

- **Future-Oriented Leadership Vision** Stanek's book critically examines the evolution of leadership theories and practices, from ancient times through the industrial revolution to the present day, offering a visionary outlook on the future of leadership. Unlike books that dwell on past or current leadership models, "The Resilient Leader, Embracing Resilience for Success" charts a course for the future, advocating for a comprehensive, adaptable leadership approach that meets the demands of an ever-changing world. This forward-thinking perspective encourages leaders to not only adapt to the new normal but to thrive within it, paving the way for a new era of leadership excellence.

In summary, "The Resilient Leader, Embracing Resilience for Success" offers a unique, comprehensive guide that goes beyond traditional leadership tenets, providing readers with the insights and tools needed to excel in today's dynamic environment. By combining a holistic view of intelligence, a focus on emotional resilience, practical tools for self-assessment, real-world applicability, and a visionary leadership approach, this book is an essential resource for anyone looking to lead effectively in the 21st century.

www.ingramcontent.com/pod-product-compliance
Lightning Source LLC
Chambersburg PA
CBHW071855160426
43209CB00005B/1059